NOT QUITE A DIPLOMAT

"A true friend and ally"
PRESIDENT CLINTON

"A remarkable Ambassador"
GENERAL COLIN POWELL

"An Ambassador with real clout in Washington"
SIR MAX HASTINGS

"Outstanding service in the US"
HENRY KISSINGER

"In the century since the British imperial statesman Sir Alfred Milner started the Boer War, no British envoy has had such an impact on South Africa as Sir Robin Renwick."
FINANCIAL TIMES

"He became a bridge between the ANC and De Klerk's government and a personal friend of Nelson Mandela."
THE GUARDIAN

"A steady, unsentimental and unfooled gaze"
ALISTAIR COOKE

"Simply the best"
RICHARD HOLBROOKE

"A masterclass in the art of diplomacy"
PROFESSOR DAVID WELSH

"No matter the Foreign Office task, Robin Renwick brought to it unsurpassed insight, rigour, tactical ingenuity and strategic vision."
SIR STEPHEN WALL

ROBIN RENWICK

NOT QUITE

A

DIPLOMAT

———

A MEMOIR

\B^b\
Biteback Publishing

First published in Great Britain in 2019 by
Biteback Publishing Ltd
Westminster Tower
3 Albert Embankment
London SE1 7SP
Copyright © Robin Renwick 2019

ISBN 978-1-78590-459-2

10 9 8 7 6 5 4 3 2 1
A CIP catalogue record for this book is available from the British Library.

Set in Adobe Caslon Pro

Printed and bound in Great Britain by
CPI Group (UK) Ltd, Croydon CR0 4YY

CONTENTS

INTRODUCTION

In June 1987, I was summoned to a reception at 10 Downing Street. Denis Thatcher congratulated me on being appointed Ambassador to South Africa. Denis, who loved playing golf with his friends in Natal, told me that I was being sent to 'God's own country'. The Prime Minister gave me her usual steely stare. 'Well,' she declared, 'at least you're not a diplomat!'

She meant this as some kind of compliment.

Harold Macmillan, walking with a friend into Downing Street, was asked which side the Foreign Office was on. 'On our side – I hope,' he replied.

Franklin Roosevelt, asked in 1942 about the attitude of the State Department, declared, 'The best that can be hoped for from the State Department in this war is an attitude of strict neutrality.'

Thatcher regarded the Foreign Office with great suspicion. It was far too eager to get on with foreigners – in her opinion, at any cost. Yet she was an ardent supporter of some of its most senior members – Nico Henderson, Michael Butler and Tony Parsons – on whom she depended critically at various points in her career.

Her attitude was the same to the civil service in general, which she regarded as an unresponsive bureaucracy, addicted to 'better-nottery'. Not long after becoming Prime Minister, she hosted a dinner with all the most senior officials, the Permanent Secretaries. Perhaps naively, believing that they too must be concerned about our woeful economic performance, she declared that, together, they could beat the system. 'But we are the system!' was the response.

Yet she depended no less critically on several of its most senior figures – Robert Armstrong, Robin Butler and Andrew Turnbull.

I did not think her suspicions were entirely unfounded. A lot of diplomacy consists of going through the motions, of making statements that are essentially meaningless, about crises no one has any intention of doing much about, apart from despatching dollops of aid to the victims. This is a tendency which has become ever more pronounced today.

Diplomats never have been very popular. They are thought to live comfortable lives abroad, dispensing hospitality at the country's expense – a travesty when I think of the hardships many of my friends have had to endure in remote and dangerous parts of the world.

Towards the end of my foreign service career, I was summoned to a meeting with the Foreign Secretary to discuss whether we should align ourselves with the Europeans or the Americans. The Foreign Office by this stage was so thoroughly Europeanised that there was not much doubt where this discussion would lead. I made the heretical suggestion that we should align ourselves with our own interests, choosing who could most practically help us attain our objectives. To be fair, this was reflected in the conclusions of the meeting, though not in the mindset of all those involved.

I had a lot of good fortune in my career. It was a period in which we did get quite a lot done, as distinct from talked about – though some of it since then has been undone, or looks like having to be done all over again. The most important lesson I learned was that nearly every crisis creates an opportunity – by forcing the participants to think the unthinkable about ways to try to resolve it. Thatcher would not have been able to force through her economic reforms but for the dire straits the country was in when she became Prime Minister. We would not have been able to get adopted an extremely risky plan for what was then Rhodesia but for the failure of all the previous half-hearted efforts and the prospect of a disastrous end to the civil war.

CHAPTER I

AFRICA IS NOT FOR THE FAINT-HEARTED

When I joined the Foreign Office, the custom was to despatch many of the best and brightest to learn Arabic at the language school at Shemlan in Lebanon, reflecting the Office's long and passionate, though generally unrequited, love affair with the Arab world. Charles Powell, who joined at the same time, found that one of his tasks in the Arabian Department was manumitting (freeing) slaves, the rule being that any serf in one of the small Gulf kingdoms who succeeded in rushing into the British embassy compound and throwing his arms around the flagstaff thereby could become entitled to his freedom.

Charles was to prove an extraordinarily important friend and ally. We worked together on Rhodesia and when, as her private secretary, he became Margaret Thatcher's closest foreign policy adviser, he helped to secure her agreement to our tactics in Europe and backing for me in South Africa. He sometimes was accused by less talented colleagues of being too influential. Very unfairly, as Charles never looked after his own interests and made a major contribution to Thatcher's successes in foreign policy.

Determined to avoid learning Arabic and, so far as possible, the Middle East, I volunteered instead to be sent to Africa, a continent the Office felt that it needed to discover, as all sorts of new countries kept bobbing up at the United Nations, freed from their colonial masters. To help discover this new universe I was despatched to Dakar in Senegal, given a Land Rover and told to find out about French-speaking west Africa.

The President, Léopold Sédar Senghor, was an ardent Francophile who, once a week, used to lecture a bemused population about the philosophical writings of Teilhard de Chardin. A civilised man, he had no ambitions vis-à-vis our tiny colony in Gambia, which Senegal entirely surrounded. When the Prime Minister was accused of plotting against him, Senghor locked him up, but sent him books in prison to improve his mind.

Boarding the ferry to cross the Gambia River, you would be ushered on to the boat by the Senegalese police in their kepis and off it by the Gambians in their khaki shorts. There, the Prime Minister told me that he would never be able to understand 'those Continentals', i.e. the

Senegalese. The British Governor was wicket keeper in the national team.

Guinea I found in a pitiable state, as they had voted against Charles de Gaulle's offer of 'cooperation' with France. The French, in response, had decamped with everything they could lay their hands on, including the tax records. The President, Ahmed Sékou Touré, maintained himself in power by numbing his people with five-hour '*discours fleuves*'.

The embassy was established on a high floor in the only skyscraper in the capital, Conakry. This was unfortunate, as there was no water or electricity. Climbing the stairs in 90 per cent humidity was an experience not soon to be forgotten. On return to London, my first recommendation was to close the embassy there, which we did.

Arriving in Accra in the Nkrumah era, I was surprised to be informed by the radio that 'the pilot of Africa has left for an unknown destination'. The Osagyefo (Redeemer) by then had become a figure of fun to the local intelligentsia. Shortly afterwards, he was overthrown. His spooky left-wing British adviser, Geoffrey Bing, had to be rescued from the wrath of the Ghanaians.

In Nouakchott, capital of Mauritania, the US Ambassador and I toasted the country's first female pilot, flying low and slow over our heads. Too slow, as it turned out, as our toast was followed by a dull thud. Arriving at the scene, we helped the young lady unharmed out of the ancient biplane embedded in the sand dunes.

Whatever might be thought of the effects of colonialism on these small, neglected countries, the effects of no colonialism were even more striking in Liberia, declared for ever a free country by the United States. Arriving in a downpour, along with my co-passengers, I was denied entrance to the terminal by a police officer in black trench coat and reflective glasses without payment of a bribe.

Our rather jaded Ambassador took me to see the Minister of Justice. 'Only,' as he observed, 'there isn't any justice.' For this was a country whose President had installed solid-gold taps in the bathrooms of his palatial mansion. The fortunes of Liberia since then have been transformed by a remarkable woman, President Ellen Johnson Sirleaf.

Back in Dakar, at the university, was an outstanding professor, the agronomist René Dumont, who wrote a seminal book, *False Start in Africa*. In it, he pointed out that the overwhelming majority of the population in the newly independent countries lived from subsistence agriculture. But the black urban elite now governing them, lawyers and professional politicians, had no interest in agriculture. They had taken over the houses and offices of the colonial rulers, but nothing much else had changed. They were, however, easily seduced by promises of industrial development that were very unlikely to be viable.

Dumont went on to become the Green candidate in the French presidential election. Operating from a barge on the Seine, his programme included no cars inside the Beltway and extending the Boulevard Saint-Michel as far as the sea! When it came to Africa, however, he knew what he was talking about.

On return to London, I became the desk officer responsible for these statelets. My writ soon extended to the former Belgian Congo, then in the throes of a civil war.

I also became a part-time resident clerk or overnight duty officer – a popular assignment, as it enabled the incumbents to seek to impress actual or potential girlfriends by entertaining them in an attic under the rafters of the magnificent building overlooking St James's Park. The messengers would bring them up in the ancient lift, the progress of which was so laborious that the American Ambassador, Walter Annenberg, declared, 'Back home, trees grow faster than this!'

One evening on duty there, I was telephoned by the Administrator of Ascension Island, who said that the airbase was full of Belgian paratroopers and the local Reuters stringer was trying to file a story about their presence.

We had agreed that the Belgians could use Ascension Island to rescue a lot of their citizens, including many women and children, trapped by the Patrice Lumumba-supporting *'jeunesse'* in Stanleyville in the Congo. Having told the Administrator to stop the Reuters stringer from filing his story by whatever means were necessary, I rolled over and went back to sleep.

Next morning the Belgians rescued their people and I was summoned to see the Permanent Under-Secretary. I had reached the right conclusion, he said, but I should have consulted someone more senior before imposing censorship on part of Her Majesty's dominions.

This was the first time I was accused of not being any good at delegating upwards, though it was not to be the last, especially by Sir Geoffrey Howe.

Not long afterwards, we received a desperate appeal for help from twelve British nuns trapped, also by the '*jeunesse*', in Albertville. This posed a dilemma, as we had no means of helping them, and the only people who did were Colonel Peters and his deputy, Major 'Mad Mike' Hoare, and their mainly British mercenaries engaged in 'pacifying' the Congo on behalf of General Mobutu. We were not supposed to have anything to do with the mercenaries, but we found a way to ask them to help, which they agreed with relish to do. Having rescued the nuns, and knowing they would not be rewarded by us, they proceeded to ransack every bank in Albertville and make off with the proceeds.

*   *   *

By this stage, the crisis in the Congo had been overtaken by that in Rhodesia, where Ian Smith was threatening to make a unilateral (and therefore illegal) declaration of independence (UDI). I joined meetings with strong, silent, square-jawed and often pipe-smoking men from the Commonwealth Relations Office to decide what to do about this. They regarded us as frightful young whippersnappers and certainly were right to do so. It took me some time to realise that some of these imposing-looking gentlemen were silent because they had nothing to say.

Any hope of averting Smith's revolt was lost when Harold Wilson, by now Prime Minister, ruled out publicly any British military response. While that certainly was his conclusion at the time, it was an act of folly to declare it publicly, as the Rhodesian commanders, many years later, confirmed to me themselves. Wilson's announcement meant that Smith no longer had to bother to consult them before declaring UDI.

Once it was declared, responsibility for Rhodesia was transferred to the Foreign Office, where we faced the thankless task of trying to persuade our friends and allies to enforce sanctions against Rhodesia as rigorously as we thought they should. To our amazement, at the Commonwealth Conference in Lagos, Harold Wilson declared that economic sanctions would end the rebellion in 'weeks rather than months'. This absurd statement was made on the advice of the recently created and soon to be abolished Department of Economic Affairs.

At this time, as I arrived each morning, entering Downing Street long before it was fenced off from St James's Park, I would encounter a tramp, kneeling on the pavement, lost in prayer, outside No. 10. There were times in this period when I felt like joining him.

CHAPTER II

JOHN FREEMAN

There followed an interlude in India, where we had a remarkable High Commissioner, John Freeman. Freeman had a distinguished war record. When, following the 1945 election, Freeman made his maiden speech in uniform, Winston Churchill shed tears that he should be doing so from the Labour benches. Starting from well to the left, as a junior member of the government he resigned, along with Aneurin Bevan and Harold Wilson, in protest at the imposition of charges on National Health Service prescriptions, the party having campaigned on the basis that they should be free.

Thereafter, he had pioneered what at the time was a new form of television, the extended in-depth interview, in his programme *Face to Face*. Unlike his latter-day successors, Freeman sat with his back to the camera, with the focus entirely on the interviewee. While remoteness was a feature of his personality, his intellectual powers were second to none. He would have been a formidably effective Foreign Secretary or Chancellor of the Exchequer.

The Commonwealth Relations Office at the time were continuing to make sporadic half-hearted efforts to resolve the Kashmir problem, bitterly disputed between India and Pakistan. The problem, as quite often around the world (it was Winston Churchill who invented Iraq), had, at least in part, been created by us. At the time of partition it had been decreed that Kashmir should remain with India, as the Maharaja of Jammu and Kashmir was a Hindu, despite the fact that Kashmir had an overwhelming Muslim majority. The result had been a local war in which India succeeded in holding on to the lion's share of Kashmir.

Each feeble British initiative to try to get talks going created expectations in Pakistan that something positive (for them) might happen, while infuriating the Indians, who were determined to maintain the status quo, as they have done ever since. John Freeman succeeded eventually in convincing Whitehall that it must cease seeking to interfere in this insoluble problem.

Freeman found it extremely difficult to get on any sort of terms with the Indian Prime Minister, Indira Gandhi. Her two closest advisers, the heads respectively of her office and of the Foreign Ministry, had views so supposedly 'non-aligned' as to be indistinguishable from those of the Soviet Union. Freeman sensibly decided that, in the longer term, this did not really matter, as India was a thriving democracy and likely to remain so.

When a Soviet defector appeared at the High Commission, I was summoned by Freeman to join him in an icy encounter with the Soviet Ambassador, who assured us that if the young man was handed back, he would come to no harm. When this failed to produce the desired result, it was followed by threats and bluster. It took us several weeks to persuade the Indian government to let him leave for Britain. My US colleagues were entitled to be a good deal more astonished when Stalin's daughter appeared at their embassy to seek refuge with them.

My duties included reporting on Kashmir, enabling me to stay in houseboats on the beautiful lakes around Srinagar, to visit the Mughal gardens at Shalimar ('If there is a paradise on earth, it is here') and, at the source of the river Jhelum, to catch some of the trout first introduced there decades before by the British Governor, Sir Francis Younghusband.

They included also attending the conferences of the ruling Congress Party held periodically in different parts of the country. On these expeditions it turned out to be essential to be armed with a case of whisky, rapidly consumed by thirsty Congressmen. My Russian counterpart would appear with a countervailing case of vodka.

John Freeman never wrote his own despatches, leaving that to me, until one day he decided to show me how it was done. There followed a limpid three-page account of all that mattered, in contrast to my more laborious efforts. I have tried to aim for brevity ever since (not always successfully).

I started to reach the conclusion that what, until then, had been pretty much a one-party system would not long stay that way, befriending the most moderate leader of the Hindu nationalist party (the Bharatiya Janata Party, or BJP), Atal Vajpayee, who seemed to me to have the makings of a Prime Minister and in due course became one.

John Freeman was transferred by Harold Wilson to become Ambassador to the United States, only for Richard Nixon, whom Freeman had denounced in the *New Statesman*, to be elected President. But Nixon reacted graciously in a potentially very awkward encounter in 10 Downing Street, declaring that some people said there was a new Nixon – and maybe there was a new Freeman! Catching up with John Freeman in Washington, I found that he had forged a close friendship with Nixon's national security adviser, Henry Kissinger, based on Henry's admiration for an intellect the equal of his own.

* * *

An overland journey by Land Rover to Kabul at New Year showed Afghanistan to be as much a geographical expression as a country, the topography rendering it impossible for any government to control much of the territory divided by dizzying mountain ranges. Travellers stopping to take photographs in the Khyber Pass were subject to shots being fired over their heads. The embassy grounds in winter had wolves at the bottom of the garden. Passage through the Kabul Gorge demonstrated how easy it had been for the Afghans in 1842 to destroy a small British army, less numerous than the troops we later sent to Helmand, leaving Dr Brydon, galloping into Jalalabad with Afghans in hot pursuit, as one of the few survivors.

CHAPTER III

GILBERT AND SULLIVAN
IN THE CARIBBEAN

Summoned at short notice back to London, I was as-
signed to be private secretary to the Minister of State,
Alun Chalfont. Previously defence correspondent of *The
Times*, he resigned subsequently from the Labour Party
in protest at the policy of unilateral nuclear disarmament.
A very engaging companion, ousted when Harold Wilson
lost the 1970 election, he wrote an entertaining article in
The Spectator. In it he declared that the Foreign Office regarded the arrival of a junior minister in much the same
way as an oyster regarded that of a grain of sand – 'the
intrusion of an irritant, with a very low probability of ever
producing a pearl'.

Well before *Yes, Minister*, he described the multiple
subterfuges the Office would engage in to ensure that no
harm was done. The Permanent Under-Secretary, Denis
Greenhill, found this amusing since, as he said to me, it

was pretty accurate. The remainder of the hierarchy professed to find it shocking, presumably for the same reason.

As Sir Alec Douglas-Home now became Foreign Secretary, Chalfont was succeeded by a Tory stalwart, Joe Godber. He drove in every day from his well-loved home base, Bedford, and really wanted to be Minister for Agriculture, an ambition he was to realise. Meanwhile, however, he was regarded by Sir Alec, rightly, as a 'safe pair of hands'.

Sir Alec, as Prime Minister, had been pilloried by the press. Yet I cannot think of any Foreign Secretary, until Peter Carrington, who was more popular and admired within the building and by his counterparts overseas. In the desperate days of Black September, when in 1970 the Palestine Liberation Organization tried to seize power in Jordan and a BOAC plane and its passengers were among the hostages captured, he coped with the crisis with calm and determination.

As Prime Minister, Ted Heath's great triumph was to negotiate us into the European Community. To Henry Kissinger's surprise and alarm, he tried thereafter deliberately to downgrade the relationship with the United States to demonstrate his *bona fides* in Europe. But the Americans trusted Sir Alec and it was largely due to his efforts in this period that relations with the US were preserved despite Heath's lack of interest in them.

* * *

There followed an episode from the works of Gilbert and Sullivan. Harold Wilson's Minister for the Colonies, William Whitlock, had been chased at gunpoint off the tiny Caribbean island of Anguilla. To reassert British authority, the Wilson government ordered an invasion of the island. The US TV channels had a field day, as they filmed the Royal Marines, with blackened faces and guns at the ready, storming ashore at dawn. There was no resistance and a British administrator was installed. Godber and I were despatched to pacify the islanders.

By the time we got there, the marines had been replaced by a contingent of the Metropolitan Police. This was a great success with the constabulary, who much preferred patrolling Anguilla in their shirtsleeves to their duties at home, and with the islanders, against whom they played a weekly game of soccer. On the day before we arrived, the match had been suspended by the referee because of foul play, only for the two teams to decide to finish it without him.

The main activity of the islanders, fishing, still was being conducted in sailing boats that looked like Arab dhows. We held a meeting with them, led by one or two engaging rogues who had chased the unfortunate Whitlock away with their pitchforks and shotguns and dreamed of attracting a casino to their beautiful, totally undeveloped island. They were revolting against our decolonisation plan to federate them with the larger neighbouring island of St Kitts, whose Prime Minister they abhorred.

We pointed out that, with a population of only a few thousand, they could hardly expect to be granted independence. They did not want to be decolonised, they declared. They wanted to be a colony of Britain, but not of St Kitts.

Our legal adviser was adamant that this was impossible. He had drafted the federal constitution for St Kitts, Nevis and Anguilla. Commitments had been entered into which could not now be broken. Britain could not be bullied by a tiny bunch of pesky islanders, who would simply have to lump it.

Godber was nonplussed. What could be done about this? I suggested changing the legal adviser, which, fortunately, did not prove to be necessary, as the suggestion sufficed to change the advice. Anguilla was declared a separate colony and has lived reasonably happily ever since.

On moving on to the Turks and Caicos Islands to stay with the Governor in a wooden house built in 1815 and therefore called Waterloo, we found ourselves obliged to wade ashore amidst a cloud of flamingos. The visit did at least result in the building of a jetty.

A visit to the British Virgin Islands proved necessary to rescind the decision of the Prime Minister to sell a lease over one of the islands, Anegada, in perpetuity to a developer.

It was with extreme reluctance that I gave up these arduous duties in the Caribbean.

* * *

Godber proved quite good at dealing with the powerful lobby of the Foreign Office Arabists, affectionately known as the camel corps. A suggestion that we should show our *bona fides* to Colonel Gaddafi, who had just taken over in a coup in Libya, by supplying him with our latest tanks, was politely turned down.

The most engaging member of the corps, the brilliant linguist James Craig, devoted his entire career to Britain's would-be love affair with the Middle East, only in his farewell despatch to make such scathing comments about those he had been dealing with that it had to be suppressed. It remains under lock and key to this day.

Other small crises followed. As we entertained him to tea, Crown Prince Fahd of Saudi Arabia started munching a sandwich. The head of the Arabian Department followed suit, only to turn to me with a face whiter than I had ever seen on another human being. 'Oh my God, it's pork,' he gasped. 'It's turkey,' I hissed.

When Sir William Luce, our Middle East envoy, returned from a mission to see King Faisal, Alec Douglas-Home asked what these meetings were like with the Saudi King.

Sir William explained that the King would sit with a semi-circle of princes and advisers behind him. As he delivered his views on the international Zionist-Marxist conspiracy, periodically he would raise his hand and say, 'Is it not so?' whereupon the advisers would assure him in a chorus, 'Indeed it is so, great King.'

Sir Alec asked if we could not behave more like the Saudi King's advisers, rather than saying, when he raised the same question, 'Well, not exactly, Secretary of State.'

The next problem arose in Oman, where the old Sultan, though now enjoying oil revenues, was declining to spend them on schools and hospitals, preferring to keep much of his treasure safe in his palace. Worse than this, he had imprisoned his son, whom we had educated at Sandhurst, in a house in the palace grounds. The Sultan's small army, the Trucial Oman Scouts, was led by British officers, who felt badly about this treatment of a fellow Sandhurst graduate.

About what happened next, we were not consulted, though it had a certain inevitability to it. The old Sultan was overthrown in a coup led by some of his own (British) officers, though not without putting up a stout resistance. We arranged an RAF plane to bring him to Britain for medical treatment. As the plane transited Bahrain, our envoy there, utterly devoid of a sense of humour, reported that the Sultan 'seemed relieved to have laid down the burdens of office'.

When the Sultan arrived at RAF Andover, my favourite

and far more senior colleague, Tony Parsons, was despatched to assure him that we had no involvement in the coup. 'As you are a man of honour, Sir Anthony, I accept your assurances,' the deposed Sultan replied, 'but I was rather surprised when Major Landon shouted through my door, "Come out, Your Majesty, with your hands up!"' The Sultan's response had been to try to open fire, but he had succeeded only in shooting himself in the foot.

*   *   *

In 1972, Sir Alec, who was an honourable man, reached agreement with the Rhodesian Prime Minister, Ian Smith, on a scheme which he believed would lead Rhodesia gradually to majority rule. The very obvious problem was that this depended on Ian Smith behaving as honourably as Sir Alec would have done. The opposition was led by Bishop Muzorewa.

I was not the resigning type, preferring to try to get policy changed. A commission including David Harlech, the former Ambassador in Washington and friend of President Kennedy, was appointed to decide whether the agreement had the support of the African population. The unsurprising conclusion was that it did not.

CHAPTER IV

'THE SICK MAN OF EUROPE'

There followed a transfer to the embassy in Paris, much appreciated by me, as my wife was French and I had studied at the Sorbonne. The embassy's reputation had suffered some ups and downs since the war. Peter Carrington enjoyed telling the story of a despatch he received from our man in Paris reporting that he had just had lunch with 'an old, broken, disappointed man who knows that never again will his country turn to him in its hour of need'.

There was more in the same vein, written after a visit to De Gaulle in Colombey-les-Deux-Églises. By the time the despatch reached Carrington, at the time in Australia, the General was triumphantly installed again in the Élysée Palace as President.

The embassy's fortunes since then had improved. The Ambassador at the time, Christopher Soames, was to become an extraordinarily kind mentor to me. A far larger than life character, his relationship with De Gaulle's successor, Georges Pompidou, had helped to pave the way for Britain's entry to what was then the European Economic Community.

Summoned immediately to lunch with him in the magnificent embassy acquired by the Duke of Wellington from Pauline Bonaparte in 1814, I found that this was a meal that could last all afternoon, ending with copious quantities of *eau de vie de poire*.

His popularity in Paris was enhanced by the no less remarkable Mary Soames, Churchill's favourite daughter and wartime commander of an anti-aircraft battery in Hyde Park. As assistant military attaché in Paris, Christopher had met her there en route to the Riviera at the end of the war. A wonderful couple, they were adored by the French, not least because, beyond all dispute, they gave the best parties in Paris, Christopher having dared to poach one of the President's chefs from the Élysée.

In June 1953, Prime Minister Churchill suffered a stroke after a dinner in 10 Downing Street. As his Parliamentary Private Secretary, Soames had combined with the Downing Street staff to pretend that the Prime Minister still was transacting business when in fact he was unable to do so – about which Christopher was entirely unrepentant – until his recovery in October. Soames moved on from the Paris embassy to become Britain's first Commissioner and chief trade negotiator for what then was still the European Economic Community.

His extremely low-profile, though bilingual, successor, Sir Edward Tomkins, could not have been more of a contrast. He did, however, adopt a sceptical attitude to some of the instructions he received from Whitehall. 'The point is, it doesn't matter,' he could be heard muttering in response to some of these, often with good reason.

The embassy was run mainly by his deputy, Christopher Ewart-Biggs. Having lost an eye in the Battle of El Alamein, he wore a black monocle, the resultant rather Bertie Woosterish appearance disguising a very sharp mind indeed. He and his wife Jane were as popular in Paris as the Soames had been. Transferred to be Ambassador in Ireland, Christopher was murdered by the IRA. We did what we could to help his stricken family, with Jane becoming a leading figure in the women's campaign for peace in Northern Ireland.

This was a period in which Britain's fortunes were at a low ebb in Europe and elsewhere. The government of Harold Wilson was engaged in a largely fictitious 're-negotiation' of our membership of the EEC, eerily foreshadowing David Cameron's efforts four decades later. Wilson, arriving in Paris to see Pompidou's successor as President, Valéry Giscard d'Estaing, wanted to know how to tell him in French that he intended to smuggle the ball out on the blind side. I was able to supply the answer (*'faire passer le ballon du côté fermé'*). But this was not an approach calculated to impress the decidedly monarchical Giscard. The 're-negotiation' of the British budgetary contribution yielded no results at all, leaving the problem to be dealt with by Margaret Thatcher.

At one of the first Group of Seven summits, convened by Giscard in Rambouillet, we found ourselves installed, by way of an office, in Napoleon's bathroom. The Prime Minister managed to struggle through his speech but, to our alarm, did not appear to know where he was. Harold Wilson resigned not long afterwards, on medical advice, suffering from early-stage Alzheimer's.

Our study of French politics was enlivened by the satirical magazine *Le Canard Enchaîné*. The *Canard* enjoyed reporting that Giscard had bumped into a milk cart in the early hours one morning, returning from an overnight assignation. France's premier Cardinal, Jean Daniélou, was reported by the Church to have died in a state of *épectase* (ecstasy), as indeed he had, but in the arms of a courtesan, thereby upholding a tradition established by the former French President Félix Faure. Those of us who frequented St-Germain-des-Prés would bump into Mitterrand entertaining attractive young ladies in the Brasserie Lipp. The French, very sensibly, reacted to all this without blinking an eye.

When Giscard succeeded Pompidou as President, he

appointed as his deputy foreign policy adviser the youthful and bilingual Jean-David Levitte. As a friend and colleague for the next thirty years, he went on to serve in every senior position in the Quai d'Orsay, as Ambassador to the US and as diplomatic adviser to Chirac and Sarkozy. Refreshingly free of the anti-American prejudices of some of his counterparts, he played a key role in the return of France to NATO under Sarkozy.

* * *

On a sunny spring morning, it fell to me to attend a display by the Royal Horse Artillery, galloping with their guns around the Tuileries Gardens. As the band struck up 'Colonel Bogey', the grizzled French veteran nearby, covered with medals, sang loudly in English the Eighth Army's version of the lyrics ('Hitler has only got one ball, Goering has two but very small' etc.). This turned out to be the legendary General Jacques Massu. As a lapsed historian, I was determined to discover what really had happened in his two most famous encounters with De Gaulle.

Massu had been first to lead his tanks into the city at the liberation of Paris. When they reached the Arc de Triomphe and his men raised the tricolore flag, shells had whistled past them from the German panzers still in the Place de la Concorde.

As the general commanding the French troops in Algeria, Massu infamously had won the Battle of Algiers by sending his paratroops into the Casbah and using methods that included torture. Massu's support from Algiers was critical in helping to secure De Gaulle's return to power in May 1958.

Summoned back to Paris when he criticised De Gaulle's plans for withdrawal, the colonists and many of his troops had hoped that he would lead a planned insurrection. When they met in the Élysée, the two old generals could be heard shouting at one another so loudly that the guards had to be told not to intervene.

De Gaulle declared that the colonists weren't really French: half of them were Spanish or Italian! Massu wanted to know what was going to happen to the Algerian soldiers (*harkis*) fighting with the French. De Gaulle banged his fist on his desk so hard that his watch splintered into fragments. Both fell to their knees to pick up pieces from the floor. Massu was placed under house arrest for a year. When the army in Algeria revolted under Raoul Salan in April 1961, Massu refused to lead the rebels.

In the most desperate period of the 1968 revolt, with Paris in a state of anarchy, the students in control of the streets, millions of workers on strike and communications between government departments cut by the telephone operators, De Gaulle simply disappeared, without telling anyone in his government. He had flown to see Massu, in command of the French Army in Germany. The French, he said, were no longer listening to him; he had been considering resigning. Massu said that if he left, it could not be in these circumstances. His troops thought nothing of the students and the Communists. They did not represent the real France.

This was the message De Gaulle wanted to hear, while his disappearance had produced the theatrical effect he had been hoping for. A massive Gaullist demonstration was held on the Champs-Élysées, featuring the veteran Gaullists François Mauriac and André Malraux, followed by elections in which the French voted in droves for order over anarchy.

In the long association between De Gaulle and Massu, it was Massu who had the last word. De Gaulle considered that this 'magnificent warrior' was not particularly intelligent. Greeted by De Gaulle with the words *'Bonjour Massu, toujours aussi con'* ('still as stupid'), Massu's reply was, *'Et toujours gaulliste, mon Général!'*

* * *

A new Ambassador appeared in the form of Sir Nicholas ('Nico') Henderson. He felt very personally the fact that, because of our economic travails and incessant strikes, we were regarded as 'the sick man of Europe'. As a result, we were being patronised by the French: nor had we been regarded any better in his previous post by the Germans. His farewell despatch on leaving Paris, leaked to *The Economist*, chronicled in graphic detail Britain's economic decline, pointing out that, if this continued, we could no longer expect to count for much in the world. Though Nico was a Whig if ever there was one, and a close friend of Roy Jenkins, this despatch caused him to be plucked from retirement by Thatcher and appointed as her Ambassador in Washington.

Transferred to the Cabinet Office in Whitehall, I was able to observe our decline at close quarters, as the government struggled to salvage the ailing state-run car, shipbuilding and steel industries with ever increasing subsidies. I joined Andrew Likierman of the Central Policy Review Staff in pointing out that it would be cheaper for us to pay all the workers at the Ravenscraig steelworks to stay at home than to pour more subsidies into the plant. We also tried, and failed, to dissuade the government from pumping huge sums into the certain-to-fail DeLorean gull-wing sports car project in Northern Ireland.

Attending the Cabinet committee on Europe gave me further insight into the world of *Yes, Minister*. Three of its members – Tony Benn, Peter Shore and John Silkin – were totally unreconciled to having anything to do with Europe and at each meeting said so in no uncertain terms, none of which prevented the secretary of the committee recording in the minutes that it had reached the conclusions set out for it in the civil service briefing note for the chairman. This was replicated in Cabinet discussions too. The Prime Minister, by now James Callaghan, decreed that there was no appeal against the minutes, thereby investing the Cabinet Secretary, Sir John Hunt, with authority akin to that of the Pope.

CHAPTER V

'A LONG-STANDING
SOURCE OF GRIEF'

In November 1978, on being appointed head of the Rhodesia Department in the Foreign and Commonwealth Office, I was told that I was being given responsibility for the most hopeless of lost causes, but also was urged by the Permanent Under-Secretary, Michael Palliser, to come up with some new ideas.

Under Foreign Secretary David Owen, efforts to do something about the problem, in concert with the Carter administration, were going nowhere because of the intransigence of Ian Smith, still in charge in Rhodesia, and the nationalist leaders with their guerrilla armies, Joshua Nkomo and Robert Mugabe. David Owen would have liked to intervene more effectively, but the Callaghan government had no intention of getting sucked into this quagmire. Rhodesia had become, in Margaret Thatcher's words, 'a long-standing source of grief' for successive British governments.

Despatched to Salisbury, now Harare, to try to talk Smith out of proceeding with elections intended to install Bishop Muzorewa, at any rate nominally, as Prime Minister, I flew there on the plane of the US military attaché in South Africa. We landed in a sharp twisting spiral, Nkomo's men having recently shot down a Rhodesian civil airliner with a surface-to-air missile.

Salisbury at the time was one of the world's most attractive small capitals, the streets lined with flamboyants, jacarandas and bougainvillea. In Meikles Hotel, the Jack Dent Orchestra played every night for all-white diners attired as in Britain in the 1940s, who were required to check their guns in at the door. The appearance of normality did not extend to the burgeoning refugee camp on the edge of town or to any of the rural areas. Travel outside the city had become extremely hazardous as daylight faded each afternoon.

While Smith remained intransigent, his deputy and Finance Minister recognised that the war was fast becoming unsustainable and the limits of white manpower had been reached. Mugabe's guerrillas had established genuine support, but also a reign of terror in the Shona-speaking areas. Any village headman opposing them was chopped to pieces in front of the villagers. The Rhodesians were responding with helicopter gunships firing indiscriminately in the villages and cross-border raids inflicting devastating damage on Zambia and Mozambique. This extremely nasty little war by this time had left 30,000 people killed.

I renewed acquaintance with Bishop Muzorewa, a decent man who, however, manifestly was not in charge. I was able to start forming a friendship with the man who by this time effectively was in charge, the charismatic and popular Rhodesian military commander General Peter Walls. Accustomed to leading his men from the front, Walls had served with the British forces in Malaya. While he was confident of a high turnout in the elections, the guerrilla forces would continue their attacks and he had no convincing plan to wind down the war.

There followed the first of many dinners at Meikles with the remarkable head of the Rhodesian Central Intelligence Organisation, Ken Flower. Each time he appeared, the band would play 'Where have all the flowers gone?' More lucid than his colleagues about their chances of survival, he understood the need for an agreement, at any rate with Britain.

At Salisbury airport, I encountered twenty young Rhodesians in wheelchairs, all victims of landmines. Outside Mugabe's broken-down headquarters in Maputo, I found a larger group of young Zimbabweans with missing limbs, the difference being that they had no wheelchairs.

There followed an uncompromising encounter with

35

Mugabe, who made clear that he had no interest in negotiations: what was needed was to get on with the war. It did not matter that his forces were losing every clash with the Rhodesians. With far greater reserves of manpower, they would win in the end.

Determined never again to have a conversation of this sort with Mugabe, I asked the embassy attaché tasked with keeping in touch with him how we could get his attention. 'They will never take you seriously', he said, 'until they are summoned to Lancaster House. They know that it is there that the independence constitutions for the other British colonies have been decided.'

In Lusaka, the vast Joshua Nkomo, full of bluster, upbraided me for the Callaghan government's failure to install him as Prime Minister of an independent Zimbabwe. It was irksome to receive these tirades from Nkomo, as he was on the payroll of 'Tiny' Rowland's company Lonrho, along with that of others. I pointed out that he might soon have to get used to dealing with Margaret Thatcher. Two days after our meeting, the Rhodesians razed to the ground the building in which it had taken place, narrowly missing Nkomo.

As a postscript to my visit, the Rhodesians discovered and told the South Africans that the US plane on which I had travelled was fitted with surveillance equipment, causing the expulsion of the US air attaché in Pretoria.

The elections duly were held, with Muzorewa winning them easily. For most of the Conservative Party the problem, self-evidently, was solved. Zimbabwe Rhodesia, as the country was retitled, now had a black Prime Minister. The Tory observer mission, led by Lord Boyd, had declared the elections free and fair. The new government should be recognised and sanctions lifted – the only problem being that no one else would do so.

We were required to submit a paper to the new Prime Minister advising her how to deal with the most immediate and difficult of the foreign policy problems confronting her. From all that I had heard and read about Margaret Thatcher, I believed that I knew exactly what she was expecting from us. This was to say that, at all costs, we must not offend the Commonwealth, or the United Nations, or the Americans by recognising Muzorewa. Sanctions must be maintained whether the Conservative Party liked it or not.

I did not believe anyway that sticking to the carcass of Anglo-American proposals which had been rejected by everyone would do anything to solve the problem. But if we recognised a Muzorewa government and no one else did, the war continued and it then went under, as I believed it would, we would have lost what remained of our reputation. We had to do better than that.

Instead we proposed that we should seek to build on

the changes that had taken place inside Rhodesia. But there would have to be major changes to the constitution, which left all real power in the hands of the whites. Once these were agreed, we should intervene directly in Rhodesia, offering new elections under British control in which all parties could participate if they chose to do so.

We also recommended that this should be an entirely British initiative. A certain amount of iron had entered into my soul about the process of agreeing joint instructions with the Americans, which, at any rate under Carter, could take weeks. In a bow to the black caucus in Congress, he had declared that the country's future army must be based on the liberation forces, thereby, in the Rhodesian view, rendering any negotiation redundant. We would need to seek support from, while not directly involving, the US (a proposition readily agreed to by Carter's Secretary of State, Cy Vance).

This extremely risky plan would never normally have been allowed to go forward by the Foreign Office hierarchy, but it was supported by my boss, Sir Antony Duff, and since all else had failed, it ended up in No. 10. As a submarine commander during the war, attacking German convoys off the Norwegian coast, Duff had suffered a depth charge attack which landed him on the bottom of the North Sea. He had to use his crew as human ballast, rushing them from one end of the boat to the other, to free up the propellers to get them afloat again.

Duff was a believer in action rather than words. Combining personal authority and good humour with a certain steeliness of spirit, he was to become a favourite of the new Prime Minister, who subsequently appointed him head of the Security Service. When, to my dismay, Duff fell ill during the negotiations, in each crisis, of which there were quite a few, I would ask myself what Duff would have done – and then try to do it.

Without Peter Carrington, by far the most remarkable of the Foreign Secretaries I served under, there would have been no Rhodesia settlement. But the first person we had to convince about this plan was Carrington himself. This very patrician figure, full of intelligence, wit, charm and wisdom, so admired by all his foreign counterparts, was not particularly popular with sections of his own party, most of whom, he knew, agreed with Lord Boyd that we should recognise the Muzorewa government forthwith. He became sufficiently exasperated by the Tory admirers of Ian Smith to point out that Smith was not the only person to have served in the Second World War, Carrington himself having done so with still greater distinction, winning the Military Cross as a tank commander at Arnhem.

Carrington agreed that we could not grant independence on the basis of a constitution that left all real power in the hands of the white military commanders. Margaret

Thatcher too was persuaded of this and, at Carrington's urging, that to be of any effective help to Rhodesia, we had to find a way to wind down the war.

At our suggestion, David Harlech was asked to check whether any of the neighbouring Presidents would recognise Muzorewa. Harlech had reported that the earlier attempt by Smith to win legal independence did not have the support of the African population.

The answer from the neighbouring governments was a resounding no. Without their support, the war would continue, and we did not believe that the regime would survive.

Margaret Thatcher set off for the Commonwealth Conference in Lusaka with all the participants convinced that we were about to recognise Muzorewa. On the plane, the Prime Minister donned dark glasses, fearing that on her arrival acid might be thrown in her eyes. Julius Nyerere, who had ruined the economy of Tanzania, made an impassioned speech urging Britain to act decisively in Rhodesia as the decolonising power, supported by Kenneth Kaunda, who had achieved similar results in Zambia, as well as locking up his political opponents there.

Thatcher enjoyed the surprise that followed when she announced that Britain did indeed plan to act decisively in Rhodesia and to hold elections under British control. To my dismay, she added that we were not going to send

British troops there, a decision we were going to have to get reversed.

So we convened a conference in September at Lancaster House. Nkomo and Mugabe were pressured into attending by their host Presidents (Kenneth Kaunda of Zambia and Samora Machel of Mozambique).

Before it started, we warned Thatcher that all the participants in it, and especially Ian Smith, would try to appeal to her. She agreed that she would tolerate no appeals. Smith's attempts, via his Tory friends, to get to see her got nowhere as, unlike them, she did not regard his rebellion against the Crown as a mere bagatelle.

Ian Smith resisted bitterly any reduction in white control. When he complained that we were stringing out the conference while people were dying in Rhodesia, this brought a nuclear reaction from the normally imperturbable Peter Carrington, who, purple with rage, told Smith that the responsibility for the war rested squarely with him.

There followed a tense and fractious meeting, which Carrington asked me to join, with the right-wing Monday Club, led by Lord Salisbury, who made clear their not very flattering views on the Foreign Secretary and his advisers. Carrington requested congratulations afterwards on having, just about, kept his temper. He followed this up with the greatest speech of his career, to his supporters and critics at the Conservative Party conference, telling them, 'We are trying to resolve a tragic problem with honour and dignity,' which earned him a standing ovation.

In meetings outside the conference, we devoted countless hours to persuading Muzorewa and his key advisers that we needed to offer elections in which Nkomo and Mugabe could participate, whether or not they then did so. In a vote on the new constitution, Ian Smith found himself in a minority of one, with Muzorewa declaring that under the existing constitution, he would indeed be a puppet.

Nkomo and Mugabe, still resisting, were told, to their surprise, that we intended, through a British Governor, to assume direct control of Rhodesia while the elections were held. My friend and colleague Charles Powell and I made repeated visits to Nkomo in his hotel suite, where he would receive us clad, bizarrely, in a raincoat. This time, we told him, we were serious, which he never had believed we were before.

There followed extremely fraught negotiations on a ceasefire, in the mornings in my office with General Walls and the Rhodesian commanders, in the afternoons with Dumiso Dabengwa and Josiah Tongogara for the guerrilla forces. Tongogara proved to be far more committed to an agreement than his political master, Mugabe. The eventual agreement was the brainchild of Brigadier Adam Gurdon of the Ministry of Defence, who, since any ceasefire without separating the forces would be bound to break down, proposed that the guerrilla forces should assemble in areas around the country under the protection of a British-led Commonwealth monitoring force.

At a crucial moment in the conference, Carrington and I crossed the road to see the Prime Minister in her office in Parliament, to ask her to push through legislation providing for us to resume direct control in Rhodesia. To bring the conference to a conclusion, we said, we would have to take the dramatic step of sending the British Governor to Rhodesia with the war still continuing and no agreement yet reached. Otherwise the intention of Nkomo and especially Mugabe was to spin it out indefinitely. Overruling her protesting parliamentary managers, she told them to get it gazetted and passed within a week.

As Governor, I had recommended Christopher Soames for this extremely risky task, though he was Carrington's choice anyway. Soames left with understandable misgivings, telephoning from his plane to tell me so. When Carrington told the British press that we were sending a Governor to Rhodesia with no ceasefire yet in sight, the response was that nothing like this had been attempted by a British government since Suez. The papers were filled with cartoons of Soames being airlifted from the roof of Government House.

The Americans, who had started off fearing that Thatcher would recognise Muzorewa, helped by joining us in lifting sanctions as soon as Soames was installed in Salisbury, making it clear to Nkomo in particular that the train was leaving the station.

As he scrambled to get aboard, Mugabe did not. In the final meeting of the conference, in a venomous speech, he rejected root and branch the entire agreement. We had expected this response from Mugabe, who had told me repeatedly during the conference that 'power springs from the barrel of a gun' and 'I have a degree in terrorism'.

But President Samora Machel's representative, Fernando Honwana, had told us that if we came up with an honourable agreement, Machel would not continue the war, which was destroying his country. At Honwana's behest, Samora Machel telephoned Mugabe to tell him to sign, failing which he would receive no more support from Mozambique.

CHAPTER VI

'ANY SELF-RESPECTING TERRORIST HAS AN AK-47'

The Lancaster House conference over, I left to join Soames in Rhodesia, only to be told that Tongogara had been killed in a road accident in Mozambique. I was and remain suspicious about this 'accident', given how closely he had worked with us and that he had negotiated a ceasefire against Mugabe's wishes.

As the British and Commonwealth monitoring teams fanned out into the remotest 'no-go' areas of Rhodesia, we passed some of the worst moments of our lives wondering how many of them would come back. In the event, all of them did, as the guerrilla forces, at first extremely suspicious, emerged from the bush. I flew around the country in a small police plane, with what looked like sticking plaster covering the bullet holes in its wings. By the end of the week, over 20,000 men had entered the assembly places, including nearly all Nkomo's forces. Mugabe had contributed as many 'mujibas', youths armed mainly with sticks, as soldiers, to General Walls's indignation. 'Any self-respecting terrorist has an AK-47,' he protested to me.

There followed weeks of extreme tension, as several thousand armed Mugabe supporters set about persuading the villagers how to vote and the Rhodesian special forces, in particular the Selous Scouts, countered with some spectacularly bloody and incompetent dirty tricks of their own.

A busload of Muzorewa supporters was shot up, ostensibly by Mugabe's forces, in reality by the Scouts. When a church was bombed, supposedly by the guerrillas, Mugabe's head of intelligence, Emmerson Mnangagwa, brought me the identity disc of the scout who had blown himself up while planting the bomb. As the election approached, an attempt was made by the South African special forces to blow up Mugabe in Fort Victoria.

Ian Smith kept trying to persuade Walls to stage a coup, which he declined to do. Doubts about my own impartiality were laid to rest as I was told of two plots against me, one by Mugabe if he failed to win the elections, the other by elements of the Rhodesian special forces who deemed me to be a bad influence on Walls. In the latter case, Flower intervened, fortunately for me.

Christopher Soames was unimpressed by the advice we constantly were given by the thousand-plus observers and press from every nation on the planet as to how better to manage the transition. 'This isn't Little Puddington in the Marsh,' he declared. 'These people think nothing of sticking tent poles up one another's whatnots.'

The only secure satellite phone we had at the time for Soames's conversations with Carrington was installed in a tent in the grounds of Government House. As Soames would explain the often very tense situation in colourful language, the military had to beseech him not to do so in his usual stentorian tones.

We got through to the elections by the skin of our teeth. The UN representative, Javier Pérez de Cuéllar, found it reassuring to find the polling stations manned by British police in their shirtsleeves. He responded to our request to declare the elections free and fair before the results were known, with Mugabe winning by a mile.

Thatcher's domestic critics were convinced that we must have assured her that Muzorewa would win, which was not the case, though the Rhodesians had believed he would. Our plan consisted of forcing the parties into a coalition, failing which there would quickly be a resumption of the war.

Before the results were declared, Duff and I were summoned to an extremely tense meeting with the Rhodesian military commanders, appalled at the outcome, with Walls declaring, 'The enemy is about to become our government.' He had sent a message to Margaret Thatcher asking her to invalidate the results. Two of his subordinate commanders were urging military action to end the process. The commander of the Rhodesian Light Infantry was expecting to be ordered to do so.

We told the commanders bluntly that they knew perfectly well that they were losing the war. While they were winning every clash with the guerrillas, they had long since lost control of the rural areas. Turning to his colleagues, Walls said, 'You know that is true.' They were obliged to admit that quite a few of their soldiers must have voted for Mugabe. The meeting morphed into a request to us to stay on to ease the transition, as Mugabe also was asking us to do.

Thatcher flatly rejected the request to invalidate the results.

She was indeed disappointed that Mugabe had turned out to be the winner, but was justifiably proud of the role Britain had played, through what she described as 'muscular diplomacy', in ending the war and bringing Rhodesia to independence in conditions far better than could have been imagined a year before. None of this would have been possible without her willingness to assume the risks of intervening directly in Rhodesia, which none of her predecessors had been prepared to do.

The Queen was represented at the independence ceremonies by the Prince of Wales. To afford a good photo opportunity, Walls had suggested that the Prince should be invited to ride on a tame buffalo of which the Rhodesians were understandably proud, buffalos being notoriously difficult to domesticate. Major Andrew Parker Bowles, who had served with distinction on Soames's staff during the ceasefire, volunteered to check out the animal, only for me to encounter him hobbling back to Government House, having been thrown off by the buffalo, which also had attempted to gore him.

As the British flag was lowered at Government House amidst a general sense of relief, I did not enjoy, any more than Thatcher did, handing this extremely beautiful country over to Robert Mugabe.

So long as there was no threat to his hold on power, apart from organising a massacre of Nkomo's supporters in Matabeleland, Mugabe governed pragmatically for two decades. Faced with the threat of losing power, he reverted to the tactics he had used to help him get there in the first place, including the murder of potential rivals, such as his former military commander, Rex Nhongo.

In August 2017, a serious attempt was made to poison his long-term deputy and principal rival of Grace Mugabe, Emmerson Mnangagwa. But this proved too much for the military commanders, who had served with

Mnangagwa in the bush war. Having clung on to power, at a catastrophic cost to his country, for thirty-seven years, Mugabe's attempt to install his wife as his successor at last precipitated his downfall.

CHAPTER VII

'THAT LITTLE ICE-COLD BUNCH OF LAND DOWN THERE'

There followed a few months of rest and recreation at Harvard, where I wrote a book about economic sanctions. This pointed out that, typically, they were imposed *faute de mieux*, the alternatives being to do nothing or to take military action. They could have the effect of weakening the targeted regime, but not of causing it to surrender if it believed its survival to be at stake. There also was an inescapable law of leakages. Properly applied, sanctions could help to change the behaviour of a regime but were very unlikely to succeed in overthrowing it. Targeted sanctions, e.g. military and financial, could be implemented more effectively than a blanket sanctions approach. The conclusion was that, beyond weakening the target, 'more ambitious claims should not be made for a sanctions policy'. As a totally unknown author, I was very surprised to find this being reviewed favourably by *Time* magazine and the *Wall Street Journal*.

As my friends and professors at Harvard all were dyed-in-the-wool Democrats, several of whom were hoping to serve in the next administration, I found myself attending a wake on election night as, contrary to most forecasts, Ronald Reagan trounced Jimmy Carter. My closest colleague there at the time was Professor Samuel Huntington, subsequently author of *The Clash of Civilisations*, which, though thoroughly disapproved of by the politically correct at the time, proved eerily prophetic about conflict in the post-Cold War world.

But the Cold War still was very much with us as I was transferred to the Washington embassy to serve as head of chancery (the political section) under Nico Henderson. In our dealings with the Reagan administration, we benefited from, and exploited, the fact that the President was known to be a well-nigh unconditional admirer of Margaret Thatcher and, if we persuaded her to ring him up, was more likely than not to agree with her. This did not apply to all subjects, but it did to quite a lot of them.

Reagan was portrayed at the time by most British commentators as a slightly backward B-movie actor, notwithstanding his record as a successful two-term Governor of California – not an easy state to govern. I ceased to underestimate him when, early in his tenure, he was asked about contradictory statements by the Defense Secretary, Caspar Weinberger; the Secretary of State, Al Haig; and the national security adviser. 'The trouble with this administration', replied Reagan with a smile, 'is the right hand doesn't know what the extreme right hand is doing.'

Also conventional wisdom at the time was that Weinberger, presiding over a huge increase in the defence budget intended to counter the Russians, was excessively bellicose, restrained only with difficulty by Haig. This was close to being the reverse of the truth. The Weinberger doctrine was that the US should carry a very big stick, to be used with extreme caution and far less frequently than the State Department would have desired. Weinberger was furious when Haig looked like embroiling the US in Lebanon.

*   *   *

From 19 March 1982, we had been trying to get the Americans to help defuse growing tension with the Argentine military junta in Buenos Aires, following the landing on the Falklands dependency of South Georgia of a group of Argentine 'scrap metal merchants'. The Americans, to our annoyance, kept insisting that they were neutral on the question of sovereignty over the Falkland Islands. Within days, the government in Britain were overtaken by a bolt from the blue.

At around midday on 31 March 1982, we received a Flash telegram containing intelligence that the Argentine Navy was at sea and planning to invade the Falklands. Nico Henderson and I went to see the Secretary of State, Al Haig, at 7 p.m. Haig was flabbergasted that his own intelligence services, with far closer contacts in Argentina, had not identified the invasion plan themselves. He agreed that Reagan must speak urgently to General Galtieri, leader of the Argentine military junta.

On the following day, my friend Lieutenant Commander Dennis Blair on the National Security Council (NSC) staff, a Rhodes scholar and future commander in chief of the US Pacific Fleet, reported that Galtieri was delaying taking Reagan's call. Should the President say that if they invaded, we would regard it as a *casus belli*? There being no time to consult the Foreign Office, who would have been bound to agonise over the reply, I said that, knowing the Prime Minister as we did, I had little doubt that we would. Blair's response was to ask how he could get a secondment to HMS *Ark Royal*.

That evening, Blair reported that when Reagan eventually got through, Galtieri appeared to have been drinking. He kept saying that 'the die is cast'. I warned the Ministry of Defence to expect an invasion in the morning.

The Ambassador, who was dining with Vice-President Bush, received the same message from him. Telephoning 10 Downing Street at 2 a.m., he found the Prime Minister, who he was convinced must have been sitting up in bed next to Denis with her hair in curlers, not at all bellicose, but understanding very clearly the gravity of the mess we were in.

The Argentinians duly landed and, to our great regret, Peter Carrington resigned. It seemed to most of us at the time that it would have made more sense for the Defence Secretary, John Nott, to go, his cuts to the navy having helped to precipitate the crisis.

My immediate assignment was to ring the Pentagon to ask that a US tanker in the South Atlantic carrying a huge quantity of aviation fuel should be diverted forthwith to our base on Ascension Island, which they agreed to do.

In Washington, our next port of call was on our closest American friend, the Defense Secretary, Caspar Weinberger. Weinberger also was a long-standing friend of Reagan and much closer to him than Al Haig.

We explained that we were going to need a great deal of military equipment to be shipped directly each night from Andrews air force base outside Washington to Ascension Island. Weinberger unhesitatingly agreed, adding that if any of our requests were declined or delayed, this must be referred to him forthwith.

He did so without consulting the State Department, which was just as well, as a struggle for influence had broken out between Larry Eagleburger, head of the European Bureau, supported by the NATO-oriented Political-Military Bureau, and Tom Enders, head of the Latin American Bureau, supported by the right-wing academic Jeane Kirkpatrick, US Ambassador at the UN. Haig's deputy, Walter Stoessel, and Jeane Kirkpatrick had actually been dining at the Argentine embassy on the evening of the invasion.

Haig, meanwhile, to Thatcher's fury, told Nico Henderson that, while his sympathies were with the British, 'the most practical expression of that sympathy would be impartial US mediation in the dispute. The honest broker must, above all, be neutral.' Haig was determined to try to act as an ostensibly neutral peacemaker.

Kirkpatrick's statement at an NSC meeting that 'Latin America is the most important place in the world for us' produced an explosion from Admiral Bobby Inman, deputy head of the CIA, who said that it was a great deal more important to support America's key allies in Europe. Reagan, as he was leaving the meeting, said that he would love to stay friends with Argentina, but 'I think that our first loyalty, if worst comes to worst, is to side with the Brits.'

Haig tried out his mediating ideas on Henderson

before setting off for London. Henderson made clear that no agreement would be possible unless the Argentinians withdrew their forces from the islands. As Haig responded that Galtieri could not survive in office if they withdrew, I pointed out to Eagleburger that the same applied to Thatcher if they didn't.

On their arrival in London, according to Jim Rentschler of the NSC staff, the US team found Thatcher 'quite fetching' in a two-piece velvet suit. Haig was accompanied by General Vernon ('Dick') Walters, who told me that as he entered the Cabinet Room the Prime Minister gripped him by the elbow, pointing out the portraits of Nelson and Wellington. 'I think I got the message,' he observed. Haig was told not to reward aggression. She had not, she said, despatched the fleet to establish some 'interim authority' but to restore British administration.

As this caravanserai moved on to Buenos Aires, the Spanish-speaking Walters had a private meeting with Galtieri, who was convinced that 'that woman would not dare' to fight for the Falklands. Walters pointed out that Thatcher had recently allowed some IRA members to starve themselves to death in British jails. 'I wouldn't count on that if I were you,' was his advice to Galtieri.

Walters was embarrassed by an article in the Argentine press suggesting that he had told Galtieri that the only thing worse than male machismo was female machismo.

Walters telephoned me to say that he had indeed said this, not as a criticism of Thatcher but as a warning.

Reagan found it hard to believe that a war could break out over what he described as 'that little ice-cold bunch of land down there'. Al Haig was bound to make every effort he could to avoid a military clash in the South Atlantic. His intentions were honourable, but, lacking Kissinger's intelligence, as he pursued his shuttle diplomacy, he seemed unable to grasp that he was trying to bridge an unbridgeable gap. He kept seeking to pretend the Argentine position was more flexible than it was. Thatcher was right to believe that he was trying to arrange a disguised transfer of sovereignty to Argentina, as Haig himself eventually confessed to the National Security Council.

Neither Henderson nor I believed that any of these efforts would succeed, as the Argentinians would not agree to withdraw from the islands or to an outcome that did not give them a guarantee of future sovereignty. Henderson was absolutely determined, however, that we must respond positively to each American initiative, it being clearly impossible for us to win the war without their support.

There were some torrid exchanges with the Americans.

To counter press reports about intelligence-sharing, Haig asked the chiefs to look at restricting the amount of intelligence that was being shared with us. Admiral

Inman told me with a smile that Haig had been assured that nothing was happening beyond the normal pattern of cooperation (which meant extensive intelligence-sharing).

Haig also wanted to declare that British use of US facilities on Ascension Island had been restricted, resulting in a stormy exchange with Thatcher, who told him, '*For Pete's sake*, get that reference to Ascension Island out of your statement, because it's OUR island.' She did not want to hear any more about even-handedness between a democratic NATO ally whose territory had been invaded and a military dictatorship in Argentina.

As we were about to reoccupy South Georgia, we felt that we must forewarn Haig. Henderson returned flabbergasted from a meeting with him, at which Haig had said that he must tell the Argentinians. Some violent remonstrances were required to prevent this happening. Thatcher was appalled.

On 22 April, Haig made his proposal to us and the Argentinians for the withdrawal of Argentine land and British naval forces from the South Atlantic and an interim administration while negotiations took place, which were supposed to result in a definitive solution by the end of the year. The Foreign Secretary, Francis Pym, recommended accepting them. Thatcher found them totally unacceptable, as they involved no return to British administration and no guarantee of respect for the wishes of the islanders.

She told her deputy, Willie Whitelaw, that she would resign if the Cabinet accepted them.

From the embassy, we had made very clear the consequences if we were held responsible for a breakdown of negotiations. We would not be able to recover the islands without American support. We did not believe that the Argentine junta would agree to withdraw their forces from the islands and nor, fortunately, did the War Cabinet. In what Henderson regarded as a 'finesse worthy of Talleyrand', Nott came up with a solution, which was to ask that Haig should first get a response from the Argentinians, who rejected them.

Henderson's bravura performance in Washington included appearing daily on the major television shows, on which he became a popular favourite, his appearance, according to the BBC, resembling that of a slightly crumbling English country house. No one could mistake him for anything other than the British Ambassador. Our air attaché also became a star on the US media, on which he would appear looking exactly like Biggles.

Henderson's efforts also included going to see every important Senator. I accompanied him at several of these meetings, my favourite being that with Joe Biden, later Vice-President under Obama. He greeted us with the words, 'Don't give me that crap about self-determination: we are going to support you because you are British!' The

Americans never were convinced that the self-determination argument could necessarily be applied to a population of 1,800 people. But the vote in the Senate ran 79–1 in our favour, the solitary dissenter being the ultra-right-wing Jesse Helms.

On 29 April, Reagan told Thatcher that he recognised that while she had great difficulty with Haig's proposals, she had not rejected them, unlike the Argentinians. Jeane Kirkpatrick reflected bitterly that 'there wasn't any question where President Reagan stood on the issue, from start to finish'.

Weinberger, who had never had any confidence in Haig's negotiating efforts, had simply been getting on with the business of making sure that we won the war.

He was so concerned about what many in the Pentagon regarded as the massive military odds against Britain that he appeared one morning at the embassy to observe (correctly) that what above all was lacking in our armoury was a large aircraft carrier. Had we thought of leasing one from the United States? Henderson and I were extremely touched by this offer, which, however, was an entirely impractical one. Amidst fervent thanks for his support, we said that we would simply have to manage with what we had got.

Late in the evening, I was summoned to the State Department by Eagleburger to receive the formal statement that there was 'reason to hope' that Britain would have considered Haig's proposals, but they had been rejected by Argentina. The United States, it said, would respond positively to requests for materiel support for Britain, thereby legitimising what Weinberger had been doing from the outset.

Following this statement, we took forthwith to Weinberger a request for the supply of 105 AIM-9L Sidewinder air-to-air missiles from the US Air Force. This was the very latest version of the Sidewinder, far more accurate than its predecessors, and not yet in service with many of America's own front-line aircraft. The head of Weinberger's office protested to me that this number of Sidewinders was more than sufficient to account for the entire Argentine Air Force. As Margaret Thatcher was to record in her memoirs, without the Sidewinders, 'we could not have retaken the Falklands'.

CHAPTER VIII

'WE HAVE CEASED TO BE A NATION IN RETREAT'

On 1 May 1982, Foreign Secretary Francis Pym returned to Washington for another meeting with Al Haig. At lunch on the embassy terrace it was disconcerting to see how much strain the jet-lagged Haig appeared to be under. He and Tom Enders had encouraged the President of Peru to put forward proposals that closely resembled his own, also with no guarantee about the wishes of the islanders. Pym was told that a military clash in the South Atlantic must at all costs be avoided.

On the following day, the British naval commanders asked the War Cabinet for permission to sink the Argentine cruiser the *General Belgrano*, which, with two destroyers, was closing in on the exclusion zone around the British naval task force. The War Cabinet had no knowledge of the Peruvian proposals; nor would it have made any difference if they had. They were following the military advice. That evening, the *Belgrano* was sunk by HMS *Conqueror*, with the loss of over 300 lives.

Haig was appalled, berating Henderson and insisting that military action must be stopped. He sent us a copy of the Peruvian plan, with a suggested ceasefire statement. Two days later, HMS *Sheffield* was sunk in an Exocet attack.

Henderson wanted amendments to the Peruvian plan referring to the wishes of the islanders. Haig was prepared only to refer to their 'aspirations and interests'. The islands were to be administered by a neutral group, with no return to British administration.

Margaret Thatcher wrote a personal letter to Reagan, which she toned down before sending it, expressing her frustration at being constantly asked to weaken her position. Nevertheless, the revised proposals were accepted, because of the need to retain US support, only for the Argentine junta again to reject any military withdrawal. In fact, it was at this point that they turned down the best prospect of an outcome favourable to Argentina.

On 13 May, Enders persuaded Reagan to try again with the Prime Minister. Enders did not lack self-confidence. As Eagleburger observed to us, 'Even though he is six foot eight inches tall, he *still* has a Napoleon complex.'

Reagan had been given the impression that the British and Argentine positions were now quite close. Thatcher disabused him. He wanted a suspension of military action, but did not think he had persuaded her. It was, she recorded, 'a difficult conversation'. Henderson could not see Reagan getting on the phone to her again in a hurry.

On 17 May, Henderson attended a meeting with the Prime Minister at Chequers to work out the final British negotiating position before the landings on the islands. Our Ambassador at the United Nations and good friend of mine, Sir Anthony Parsons, with whom I had kept in touch throughout the crisis, also was at this meeting. Tony Parsons had told me that, a few days before, the Prime Minister had said to him, 'It is going to be the most awful waste of young life if we really have to go and take those islands.'

In the meeting, Henderson reported, he and Parsons were accused by Thatcher of being 'wet' and unsupportive of British interests. Nevertheless, she accepted the idea of UN administration of the islands.

This was such a distance from where she had set out that Parsons felt obliged to check with her that she really understood what she had agreed to. Henderson observed that what the Americans respected most was success. No diplomatic problems would matter much in the event of success, which Admiral Lewin was confident of achieving.

When these proposals too were rejected by the junta, the UN Secretary General, Javier Pérez de Cuéllar, abandoned his attempt at mediation.

At 4 a.m. on 21 May, our forces began their landings in San Carlos Bay, with very limited air support. Early that morning, the Pentagon contacted me to say that they had news of landings. They presumed that these were further commando raids. I did nothing to discourage that belief. Two or three hours later, the Argentine Air Force started launching their attacks on the landing ships, which, nevertheless, succeeded in getting the entire landing party ashore. Over the next few days, the navy lost HMS *Ardent*, *Antelope* and *Coventry*, as well as the *Atlantic Conveyor*, carrying helicopters and other heavy equipment for the landing force. *Argonaut* and *Brilliant* were badly damaged. The Harriers armed with the US Sidewinder missiles caused heavy losses among the attacking aircraft.

My friends in Foggy Bottom (site of the State Department) warned us that Haig was preparing yet another initiative. Henderson told him that, having had to fight our way ashore, we were not going to withdraw and nor was there any longer going to be an interim administration.

Before President Reagan left for a Group of Seven summit in Versailles, Jeane Kirkpatrick met him to say that a bloody British military victory in Port Stanley would destroy the US position in Latin America.

Haig once again summoned the Ambassador. I accompanied Henderson to the meeting, having been forewarned that Haig would be quoting Churchill to us about magnanimity. When he did so ('In Victory, Magnanimity'), we replied that Churchill had been talking about magnanimity *once victory had been achieved*. We added that, as a soldier himself, surely he could understand that we could not tell our military, who had suffered serious casualties, to stop fighting on the verge of victory.

Nevertheless, prompted by Haig, Reagan telephoned the Prime Minister again on 31 May. He congratulated her on 'what you and your young men are doing down there', demonstrating to the whole world that aggression does not pay. But he then sought to urge her that a deal should be struck to avoid 'total Argentine humiliation'.

He was unable to get much beyond the word 'Margaret…' in the rest of the call. 'This is democracy and *our* islands,' she told him. Having lost valuable British ships and invaluable British servicemen's lives to return to the Falklands, there was no longer any question of an interim administration. She was sure that he would have reacted in the same way if, say, Alaska had been threatened. Reagan protested feebly that Alaska was different, but she did not agree. 'There is no alternative,' she concluded.

The NSC staff felt that in this call, Reagan had sounded like more of a wimp than Jimmy Carter. Reagan recorded afterwards that she had said that too many British lives had been lost 'and she convinced me'.

Reagan's heart was not really in some of these calls. One

of those present in the Oval Office told me that during this diatribe, the President, unable to get a word in edgeways, held up the phone to his staff. 'Isn't she wonderful?' he said.

A cross Thatcher telephoned Henderson on an open line to say that she was 'dismayed' by the President's attitude, which had 'horrified' her. 'We have lost a lot of blood,' she said, 'and it's the best blood.' Haig was equally dissatisfied, telling Henderson, 'We can't accept intransigence.'

As our forces closed in on Port Stanley, Britain and the US vetoed a resolution at the UN calling for an immediate ceasefire. No sooner had the vote been taken than Jeane Kirkpatrick caused a minor sensation by saying that if it were possible to change votes, she would have recorded an abstention. To Thatcher's amazement, Reagan knew nothing of what had transpired.

In his speech to the Houses of Parliament a few days later, Reagan aligned himself firmly with the Prime Minister. With the war not yet ended, British soldiers in the Falklands, he said, were fighting not for mere real estate: 'They fight for a cause, for a belief that armed aggression must not be allowed to succeed.'

On 14 June, news of the Argentine surrender was greeted with cheering in the Operations Room of the White House. Margaret Thatcher declared, 'We have ceased to be a nation in retreat.' For all her annoyance with Haig and at their constant attempts at mediation, the United States was bound to have tried to play a peacemaking role. Haig himself concluded that the fatal Argentine miscalculation had been about the character of the British Prime Minister. The British had shown that they were prepared to fight for a principle and to do so supremely well against considerable odds. The Argentine military were discredited and the pressures for democracy strengthened.

Haig's successor, George Shultz, regarded the British decision to go to war for these desolate, scarcely populated islands 8,000 miles from London as an important statement that a free world nation was willing to fight for a principle. The world paid attention to this. The Soviets, in his opinion, did so too, a view corroborated by Christopher Meyer, then in Moscow, who found his Russian contacts taking a keen interest in the emergence of this new *tsarina*.

Shultz was soon to make very clear, however, that the US was not prepared to be pushed around by Thatcher over its future policies in Latin America.

CHAPTER IX

THE 'ZERO OPTION'

My main task in the embassy was liaison with the Political-Military Bureau in the State Department and their counterparts in the Pentagon about Cold War issues and arms control. The Bureau, led by Richard Burt, subsequently US Ambassador in Germany, contained an extraordinary array of talent at the time – Bob Blackwill, David Gompert, Richard Haass and James Dobbins, all of whom went on to much more senior positions. These contacts had proved very useful during the Falklands War.

In the Pentagon, Cap Weinberger, while the staunchest of allies, was a sceptic about arms control, pointing out to me that neither of the Strategic Arms Limitation Talks (SALT) agreements so far reached with the Russians had resulted in any reduction in nuclear weapons; they had simply set ceilings above what both sides had already. His Assistant Secretary, Richard Perle, known to the British press for his hardline views as 'the Prince of Darkness', did not believe in arms control at all and was well equipped with quotations from Churchill about the dangers of sitting down with crocodiles.

The burning issue in these years was the decision of Britain, Germany, Italy and the Netherlands to agree to the deployment of new US intermediate-range missiles on their territory to counter the aggressive deployment by the Russians of SS-20 nuclear missiles targeted on western Europe.

The missiles for Britain were intended to be deployed at Greenham Common, where a large women's peace camp had been formed to oppose the deployment. The Soviet calculation very obviously was that, with any luck, the deployment would become politically impossible in western Europe.

The Americans had appointed as their negotiator Paul Nitze, a veteran of the Cold War. I had met him before his appointment and his future (second) wife also was a friend. Having made a fortune at Dillon Read before the war, he had served in nine different administrations, including under Kennedy. He was a critic of SALT II because it left in place all the huge Soviet land-based SS-18 missiles, which, in their fixed silos, were so vulnerable to attack in a crisis as to risk creating a 'use it or lose it' psychology on the part of the Russians.

Immediately after his appointment, I had lunch with Nitze at the Maison Blanche restaurant just outside the

White House. I said that for the Thatcher government to go ahead with the deployment in the face of largely hostile public opinion depended on our demonstrating that we were doing everything possible to negotiate in good faith – and that in turn depended on our really doing so. Paul Nitze said that we need have no fears on that score and was to prove as good as his word.

The main architect of the US position turned out be Richard Perle, who proposed that the maximum number of intermediate-range missiles on both sides should be zero!

This produced a major fit of the vapours in Whitehall, where, understandably, it was held to be non-negotiable. I tried to reassure my colleagues that if, in the end, equal limits were agreed, I was sure the US would accept that.

After months of frustration at stonewalling by the Soviets and at his own hardline instructions (zero missiles on either side) from Washington, Nitze invited his Soviet counterpart, Yuri Kvitsinsky, to a 'walk in the woods' in which Nitze, without instructions, offered the obvious solution of equal numbers of missiles on each side. This was rejected by the Russians, who still hoped to prevent the western deployment altogether.

At this point, I contacted Perle to say that I had an extremely sensitive matter to discuss. Perle, characteristically, said that, in that event, we could not possibly meet in the Pentagon. He proposed a sushi bar nearby instead.

We duly met there, in a suitably private booth. I said that if we sought to move the missiles into the base by road, there would be a serious risk of casualties as peace campaigners lay down in the roads. Instead, we wanted the US to airlift the missiles directly into the base on their huge C-5 Galaxy transport aircraft – an idea that could not possibly fail to appeal to Perle.

The missiles duly were delivered to Greenham Common. The Russians, as expected, broke off the negotiations, which they had ensured were going nowhere. In due course, also as expected, the talks were resumed, but this time with the missiles deployed on both sides. In 1987, under Mikhail Gorbachev, the Intermediate-Range Nuclear Forces (INF) agreement was signed, one of the first real measures of arms control, abolishing intermediate nuclear weapons on both sides – the zero option. The INF agreement since has been jettisoned by Vladimir Putin, developing hundreds of intermediate-range nuclear weapons in violation of the treaty, in pursuit of the dangerous notion of 'escalation dominance' in the event of any conflict in Europe.

*   *   *

Immediately after the G7 summit in Versailles, Reagan visited Britain. He stayed and went riding with the Queen at Windsor, which he described as 'a fairy-tale experience'. It had been suggested that he should address a joint session of Parliament in Westminster Hall, but this was vetoed by the Labour Party. Instead, he addressed those Members of Parliament who wished to hear him in the Royal Gallery.

Reagan had thought hard about his speech, on which he was helped by his speechwriter Peggy Noonan, seeking to encapsulate his philosophy. He saw the world as at a turning point. Marx was right that they were witnessing a revolutionary crisis, in which economic demands were conflicting with those of the political order. But the crisis was happening not in the west, but in the cradle of Marxism. It was the Soviet Union that was running against the tide of history. It was in deep economic difficulty. The advance of freedom and democracy would leave Marxism-Leninism on the ash heap of history. The determinant in this struggle would not be weapons, but the clash of wills and ideas.

The phrase about the 'ash heap of history' was borrowed from Trotsky. The majority of British and American commentators were far too sophisticated to fall for what they regarded as this crude anti-Soviet rhetoric. There was far more interest in his use of a British invention, which he had introduced to Margaret Thatcher – the autocue.

* * *

Thatcher's hopes that US sanctions against Russia over Poland might be eased were confounded when they were in fact intensified. Reagan regarded this as an entirely justified reaction to the suppression of Solidarity in Poland. Thatcher was indignant at their impact on British companies, in particular the engineering company John Brown. To keep American farmers happy, the US had decided to lift its ban on the sale of grain to the Soviet Union, which she regarded as hypocritical.

When she visited Washington on 23 June 1982, eight days after the victory in the Falklands, the US side mentioned that they had been talking to John Brown, who did not seem too concerned, provoking an angry response from Thatcher: 'You deal with *your* companies and I will deal with mine.' One month later, the British government used its legal powers to prohibit John Brown and US subsidiaries in Britain from complying with the US embargo. In November, Reagan announced that he was abandoning the attempt to apply the sanctions extraterritorially.

CHAPTER X

'THE BRITISH GOVERNMENT HAD BEEN MADE TO LOOK IMPOTENT'

Next, we encountered another storm from a blue Caribbean sky. On 13 October 1983, the crypto-Marxist regime of Maurice Bishop in Grenada was overthrown in a coup. Six days later, Bishop was murdered.

The Reagan administration had strongly disliked the Bishop regime, with its close ties to Cuba and several hundred Cuban construction workers in Grenada building a large new airport. They would dearly have liked to get rid of Bishop, but not in the way that had now happened, for Bishop was overthrown by a group of extreme left-wing thugs, led by General Hudson Austin. The Governor General and representative of the Queen, Sir Paul Scoon, was powerless to do anything. Several hundred American students were present on the island at the time.

The Americans consulted the Foreign Office as to what should be done. They were told that Grenada was independent. The coup had taken place and there was nothing that could be done about it, despite the unpleasant nature of the regime. The effect of this uncompromising reply was to ensure that we were excluded from US planning.

For this was not the view taken by the other Caribbean leaders, who feared that they might be next. The Prime Minister of Barbados, Tom Adams, and the redoubtable Eugenia Charles, Prime Minister of Dominica, appealed to the Foreign Office, with no success, and to the United States for help.

US naval vessels were diverted, ostensibly to assist with the evacuation of US citizens. On Friday 21 October and through the weekend, I and others in the embassy asked the State Department about US intentions. We were told that the US was proceeding cautiously. No decisions had yet been taken. If they were, we would be forewarned.

In fact, President Reagan had been woken up at the Augusta Golf Club on the Saturday morning to be informed of the Caribbean leaders' request for US intervention. He agreed that planning should be carried forward.

Back in Washington on the Sunday morning, he was told of a Hezbollah attack on the US Marine Corps barracks in Beirut in which 241 marines were killed. The National Security Council met throughout the morning.

There was a sense of intense frustration at the inability to take any effective retaliatory action. When the meeting turned to Grenada, Reagan declared himself in favour of intervention. Otherwise, he said, the US people might just as well have re-elected Jimmy Carter.

By the Sunday evening, I suspected that the US might be heading in that direction. A senior State Department official told me that Grenada was now a subject on which there was 'no cable traffic'. First thing in the morning, I asked the Ambassador, Sir Oliver Wright, to contact Larry Eagleburger, by now Under-Secretary of State. Eagleburger confirmed that the US was now heading in the direction of intervention.

Because of the time difference, this report did not reach London in time to prevent the Foreign Secretary, Geoffrey Howe, declaring in Parliament that he had no reason to believe that the US were considering intervening – a statement based on the prior reporting, but not checked with us before he made it.

That evening, the Prime Minister received a message from Reagan saying that he was seriously considering the request from the Caribbean leaders for the US to intervene. She remained strongly opposed. Reagan tried to contact her, but found that she was out – at a dinner with Princess Alexandra, attended also by the US Ambassador, who knew nothing of his government's intentions. On her return to Downing Street, she received a second message, confirming the US intention to intervene. She replied immediately, opposing intervention in the affairs of a small independent country, 'however unattractive its regime'.

She followed this up with a call to the White House, where the President was briefing the Congressional leaders. Called out of the meeting, Reagan spoke to her for fifteen minutes. She expressed in her usual uncompromising terms her opposition to US intervention in an independent Commonwealth country. Reagan was taken aback. He had expected her to be better disposed, whatever the attitude of the Foreign Office. But he was not deterred. The US intended to act in support of the Caribbean leaders.

Margaret Thatcher felt badly let down. 'At best, the British government had been made to look impotent; at worst we looked deceitful.' Now she and Geoffrey Howe would have to explain 'how it had happened that a member of the Commonwealth had been invaded by our closest ally'.

That night, a US Navy SEAL team was put ashore and managed to reach the Governor, Sir Paul Scoon, whom they found in fear for his life. He signed a letter requesting US military intervention. Despite some Cuban resistance, within a few hours, the US had gained control of the island.

In Parliament, the opposition had a field day. The US action was deemed to be particularly heinous because

Grenada was a member of the Commonwealth. This despite the fact that we had refused to intervene ourselves and the Americans had been greeted as liberators by the people of Grenada, thankful to have been rescued from a bunch of thugs who had seized power illegally.

The Americans saw themselves as carrying out responsibilities that Britain hitherto had exercised in helping to provide for the security of the small island territories in the Caribbean. They had intervened in the area before and were to do so again, in Panama and Haiti.

George Shultz was himself partly responsible for the failure to consult us earlier. But he and Reagan were convinced that on this issue the Prime Minister was 'just plain wrong'. As Margaret Thatcher was about to speak in the parliamentary debate on the issue, Reagan telephoned her to try to make his peace. She was uncharacteristically muted in her reply.

She told the Cabinet she was convinced that she had been right to oppose intervention and remained of that opinion when I pointed out to her, years later, that the US intervention had worked out a great deal better for the people of Grenada than the alternative would have done. But, she concluded, the United States had taken a different view on an issue that directly touched its national interests: 'Britain's friendship with the United States must on no account be jeopardised.' Geoffrey Howe, an ardent

European, felt that 'Grenada, rather than the Falklands, offered the best evidence of American instincts'. In the Washington embassy we were left licking our wounds at the failure to forewarn him in time.

CHAPTER XI

'GETTING OUR MONEY BACK'

Transferred to the Foreign Office in April 1984 as the Under-Secretary responsible for negotiations with the European Community, the burning issue was the British budgetary contribution to the EC, which far exceeded the payments we received from it, and which the Harold Wilson 're-negotiation' had failed to do anything to correct. Nor had Margaret Thatcher as yet been able to achieve anything approaching a permanent solution. The negotiations appeared to be well and truly deadlocked. At the European Council in March, Helmut Kohl had offered a flat-rate rebate of 1 billion ecus (European currency units), rejected by Thatcher as totally inadequate.

Our negotiating position was based on a Treasury paper which contended that a country with below-average GDP, like Britain at the time, should make no net contribution at all. Thereafter, there would be a fiendishly complicated sliding scale. Visits to Brussels and other European capitals convinced me that this scheme had no chance of success. While most of the other governments had never even studied it, they were unanimous in their determination to have nothing whatever to do with it.

As the French held the presidency of the Community, one of my first tasks was to accompany Margaret Thatcher to Paris for a meeting with President Mitterrand. In opposition, Mitterrand had been the leading critic of the constitution of the Fifth Republic as giving too much power to the presidency. It was entertaining to see the transformation of this consummate politician, whom I had seen in the days when he was enjoying a bohemian lifestyle on the Left Bank. Now there he was, installed in the general's office, enjoying all the trappings of the De Gaulle presidency. What remained reassuringly familiar was the team of attractive and efficient young women on his staff.

Her tête-à-tête meeting with Mitterrand over, on the plane back to London Margaret Thatcher was pessimistic about the chances of any progress on the budgetary problem. But David Williamson, head of the European Secretariat in the Cabinet Office, and I had come away with a more positive impression from our discussions with Mitterrand's key advisers. Because of the history of Gaullist obstructiveness and an adversarial relationship between our delegations in Brussels, where they were described as carrying on the Hundred Years War by other means, the tendency on our part generally had been to try to enlist the support of the other member states against the French. This had never met with much success. We believed that, on the contrary, the best chance of success lay in doing a deal with the French, then bouncing the others into accepting it.

For, at the time, the most difficult of the allies we had to deal with were the Germans. While the French knew their minds, my colleagues in Bonn never seemed to be able to make up theirs. With straight faces they would tell us that, on the one hand, they were opposed to any reform of the Common Agricultural Policy (German farmers having prospered greatly from it) but that, on the other, there must be no increase in the Community budget, and certainly not in the German contribution to it. After these sessions with our colleagues in Bonn, one scarcely knew whether to laugh or cry.

Matters were made worse by the lack of any empathy between the Prime Minister and Helmut Kohl, who on one occasion hid in a cake shop rather than prolong a meeting with her. For their security, the Germans looked to the United States; for their legitimacy, to 'Europe' and to France. In their calculations, Britain came a bad third.

So we spent many hours in discussions with our French

colleagues, Guy Legras and Elisabeth Guigou (later to become Minister of Justice). For Williamson and I had concluded that we needed to adopt a radically simplified solution, based on a two-thirds abatement of the difference between what we contributed to the Community budget and what we received, provided this was made a permanent mechanism, enshrined in Community law and changeable, therefore, only by unanimity.

When we tried this on Geoffrey Howe, the response was that we could try to negotiate something on those lines, but on our heads be it if the Prime Minister didn't like it. Geoffrey Howe did not enjoy arguing with the Prime Minister, for which he could hardly be blamed, as she was often rude to him. 'I know what you are going to say, Geoffrey,' was how she was reported to have begun one meeting with him, 'and the answer is no.' It was made very clear to us that this was an argument we were going to have to conduct with her ourselves.

So the scene was set for the European Council in Fontainebleau in June. The motorcade whisked the Prime Minister and us from Orly airport to the château. She was greeted in the courtyard by Mitterrand and a full guard of honour in their magnificent uniforms. The French, as she observed, know how to do these things properly. There was a round of applause from the bystanders. Although hardly a favourite of the French press, she always got a friendly reception from the French public, as a highly recognisable *monstre sacré*. The other heads of government were, to them, indistinguishable one from the other, apart from the massive Chancellor Kohl.

Thatcher got on well with Mitterrand, infinitely preferring him to his aloof and chilly predecessor, Giscard d'Estaing. He had established a mildly flirtatious relationship with her ('He likes women,' as she observed), which worked because he had proved himself to be an ally when it counted, during the Falklands War. It was his close friend and the Minister for Europe, Roland Dumas, who claimed that he had described her as having 'the eyes of Caligula and the mouth of Marilyn Monroe'. She always wore a more than usually elegant suit for these encounters with the French; nor was there ever a blonde hair out of place.

That afternoon, to her frustration, was spent discussing the state of the world economy. At last they got to the European Community budget. She told the others that she was not prepared to accept any more temporary solutions to the British budgetary problem. There was going to have to be a permanent solution. Mitterrand referred the matter to the Foreign Ministers to discuss that evening, before launching into an account of his recent visit to Moscow.

She found this intensely frustrating, as she made very clear to those of us accompanying her en route through the forest of Fontainebleau to the Hôtellerie du Bas-Bréau near the village of Barbizon, a favourite haunt of Robert Louis Stevenson and numerous French artists and writers from the end of the nineteenth century. Here, the heads of government and Foreign Ministers were due to have their two separate dinners. On this warm summer evening, we waited on the terrace for her to emerge. Ever meticulous, she had kept the menu, revealing that they had dined on foie gras, lobster, rack of lamb and raspberry soufflé.

To her extreme annoyance, the Foreign Ministers' meeting had proved to be a fiasco. We had not expected much better, with the small and pompous French Foreign Minister, Claude Cheysson, as chairman.

In an attempt to woo him, Geoffrey Howe had used his favourite tactic of inviting him to spend a weekend at the Foreign Secretary's beautiful country house at Chevening. The visit had not been an unqualified success, as I had to help M. Cheysson to extricate himself from the maze, where he was not tall enough to see over the hedges.

The Foreign Ministers had wasted most of their time listening to Cheysson's own account of world affairs. On the budget issue, they had simply 'clarified the points of difference', with Cheysson suggesting that we might get between 50 and 60 per cent of our net contribution back. When this was reported by Geoffrey Howe to the Prime Minister, sitting with us on the terrace of the hotel, she exploded with rage. 'How dare they treat Britain in this way?' she stormed. 'Have they forgotten that we saved all their skins in the war?'

She was upset that the Treasury's scheme, whereby our contribution would be based on relative prosperity, had been rejected by everyone. I said that I doubted if the Treasury scheme was best for us anyway. With Greece and Italy already in the Community, Spain and Portugal about to join it, and the improvement in our own economic performance, it could work against us over time. David Williamson, her trusted adviser from the Cabinet Office, and I told her that we still believed we could work things out with the French. We were told to go and try.

As it was by now past midnight, we set off to rouse my French counterpart, Guy Legras, from his hotel. We agreed with him a text providing for the permanent correction of our contribution as it was to be embodied in Community law and changeable only by unanimity. But we left the percentage figure blank.

Legras said that Mitterrand would not go above 60 per cent. We told him that there would be no settlement at less than two thirds of our contribution back. But having learned something by this time of Margaret Thatcher's psychology, we were determined to leave it to the Prime Minister herself to set the final figure. Otherwise she would never accept that it was the best that could have been achieved.

Next morning, she felt that we had shown the 'brains and determination to retrieve something from this debacle'. We knew that, behind the scenes on the French side, we were being helped by Roland Dumas, Cheysson's deputy, soon to be his successor and much closer to Mitterrand. The most distinguished of French left-wing lawyers, disentangler of the Picasso inheritance, he was the epitome of *'gauche caviar'* (members of the French left with expensive tastes), with a private life colourful even by French standards. But he was a born negotiator. It was Dumas who had urged us to find a new approach. We knew that he wanted an agreement, as did Mitterrand's key assistant, Elisabeth Guigou, whose influence with her President may have been helped by the fact that she combined beauty with intelligence.

In the European Council meeting, the Prime Minister was accompanied by Geoffrey Howe and by the 'combative and cerebral'* Michael Butler, who, as our Ambassador to the European Community, had done much to pave the way for success. The text we had agreed with Legras was circulated to the heads of government.

There followed an acrimonious debate, with the Prime Minister insisting on a 70 per cent reduction in our contribution and the others rejecting it. When an exasperated

---

* Nigel Lawson's description

Mitterrand finally proposed 65 per cent, she said that he could not refuse her one percentage point more, then called a time-out. Emerging from the meeting, this was the time to settle, she felt. With considerable relief, we agreed.

The Germans, outmanoeuvred, were going to have to foot most of the bill. Hans Tietmeyer, then in the Finance Ministry, was especially cross. But, as we had hoped and anticipated, Helmut Kohl was not prepared to veto an agreement negotiated with the French.

In financial terms, it is hard to think of a more valuable agreement having been negotiated by any British government. What we negotiated was an abatement, not a rebate of our contribution: we did not have to wait to get the money back. It has saved this country billions in every subsequent year of our membership of the European Community, then Union – even after Tony Blair subsequently sacrificed half our budgetary correction in response to pleas from others to facilitate the entry of the eastern European countries into the EU.

The Fontainebleau agreement pretty well ended for a while the argument as to whether we should remain members of the European Community. Anyone suggesting that, once having left, we should consider rejoining the EU will need to realise that the budgetary correction will lapse with our exit, and it would be very unattractive to rejoin without it.

This outcome could never have been achieved without the ferocious determination and intransigence with which the Prime Minister pursued her goal. She succeeded, however, at a severe cost to her relationships with the others.

Not long afterwards, standing with her in a window at Chequers, I found her gazing at a landscape of yellow oilseed rape, planted with subsidies from the European Commission. 'This used', she hissed, 'to be a green and pleasant land!'

CHAPTER XII

'WE DECIDED TO GIVE THE GO-AHEAD FOR THE CHANNEL TUNNEL'

In December 1984, we all reassembled in the Cabinet Room for the usual set-piece meeting with the Prime Minister before a further summit with Mitterrand. As our Ambassador in Paris was left off the attendance list, I asked Charles Powell, private secretary to the Prime Minister, to get him included, which he did. Our envoy, unfortunately, sat through the meeting without saying a word, causing Thatcher to ask what was the point of inviting him.

These large set-piece meetings around the Cabinet table before each important European meeting had become a ritual with her. At this stage of her Prime Ministership (but less so later), she would wade overnight through every page of the voluminous material provided for her.

Each of us then would be subjected to an inquisition

about its contents. Officials summoned to these meetings who had not attended them before found the experience frankly terrifying. Her ministers did not enjoy them either. She would glare around the room, expecting most of her advisers to be afflicted with terminal dampness, verging on treason.

As Michael Butler observed, these encounters were not for the faint-hearted. It was from him that I learned how to cope with the Prime Minister. For we never found that she resented argument. It was in fact her way of making up her mind. The key was to look her straight in the eye, to be even better prepared than she was – and then to stand our ground. With members of the mandarinate she trusted – a trust that had to be earned – she knew that there would be no press leaks the next day. Nor was it ever true that she did not change her mind. She did so far more often than she admitted – provided she was convinced that the persuader had the same objectives. She had little patience for those who, when challenged, did not argue back.

A debate had been going on for years about plans for the Channel Tunnel, with no perceptible progress whatever. On this occasion, the discussion was opened by the Transport Secretary, Nicholas Ridley, who made clear that he was against it, not on any technical or financial grounds, but in principle – for, apparently, visceral reasons. This, at the time, was thought to be the attitude of the

Prime Minister as well. An official from his department was subjected to a fearful inquisition. Why could there not be a bridge instead? What was the point of a tunnel if she and Denis could not drive through it? And so on.

Margaret Thatcher's main concern, however, was her very accurate suspicion that the project would cost far more than the contractors were telling us and that, when this happened, the government would be asked to foot the bill. Michael Heseltine was in favour of public funding. After all, he pointed out, we funded tunnels under the Mersey. Whatever one thought of this argument, it was the one least likely to appeal to her.

Geoffrey Howe, for all his pro-Europeanism, was against the project, because of the impact he feared the through traffic would have on his constituency in Surrey. So as the Prime Minister started to gather her papers, the lonely task of arguing for it was left to Michael Butler, supported by me. 'But I thought this was a Conservative government,' he said. Whatever we thought of the financial projections, the banks had undertaken to fund the project themselves. How could it be compatible with her philosophy to prevent them from doing so? I pointed out the advantages to British exporters of being able to freight shipments through the tunnel to many of their main export markets overnight. This earned us a basilisk stare.

The meeting ended with no indication that she had reached any conclusion, as we all trooped off with her to the meeting with Mitterrand in Paris. That evening, when she returned to the embassy from her private dinner with Mitterrand, she gave us her usual meticulous account of what had happened, on every other subject. At the end of which, she announced casually, 'And by the way, we decided to give the go-ahead for the Channel Tunnel,' producing a strangled cry from Geoffrey Howe, whose worries about his constituency were cheerfully brushed aside.

When it came to the ground-breaking ceremony in France for work on the Tunnel, she was determined to surprise Mitterrand by bursting into French. With her usual intensity, she practised with ferocious concentration with my wife, delivering her speech in an accent described by *Le Monde* as '*plus qu'honorable*'.

CHAPTER XIII

'I WOULD BE AFRAID THAT
SHE MIGHT POISON ME'

After the bruising encounters over 'getting our money back', the European Commission under Jacques Delors was determined to give some new impetus to European integration. We ourselves wanted to see faster progress with the directives needed to achieve a genuine common market. Such a market existed so far as material goods were concerned, but not in services, in areas like insurance, air services and the professions, where our competitive advantage lay.

The Commission, including Margaret Thatcher's appointee in charge of the single market, Arthur Cockfield, argued that, to enable faster progress to be made and to prepare for further enlargement, the treaties should be amended to provide for more majority voting. The Prime Minister was strongly opposed to amending the treaties, which she saw as opening Pandora's box.

We circulated a paper arguing for a genuine common market in the service industries and the professions. In foreign policy, we were determined to maintain our own freedom of action and so were the French, but we did want better consultation among the Europeans. This was included in the paper as well. Copies were given in confidence to the foreign policy advisers to Mitterrand and Kohl.

As we walked across Downing Street to the meeting with the Prime Minister preceding the Milan European Council in June 1985, we learned that Mitterrand and Kohl had circulated our paper to the other member states proposing that this, together with the existing treaties, should constitute 'European Union'. As Margaret Thatcher observed, it was the kind of behaviour that would have got you thrown out of any London club.

Accompanying her to international meetings was always a challenging experience, due to her determination to be the best-prepared head of government in the room. She would emerge from each dinner with her counterparts, kick off her shoes, seize a stiff whisky and give us a detailed and often hilarious account of what had transpired, while discussing tactics for the next day.

The meetings never failed to offer a comparative study in national characteristics, with Helmut Kohl personifying Germany, the Belgians and Luxembourgers (even then, Jean-Claude Juncker) extremely reluctant ever to stand up to the French, Garret FitzGerald and Charles Haughey representing the two very different faces of Ireland, the Italians also appearing to be typecast and Ruud Lubbers ruggedly independent for the Dutch. The French, having very effectively colonised the European Commission, pursued their objectives with what they cheerfully described to me as 'sacred egoism'. The British delegation, so often the odd men out, must have appeared as much of a caricature of ourselves as any of the others.

We operated at a disadvantage in some respects. The southern member states would sign up to directives, for instance on environmental controls, with no intention of showing any great urgency in implementing them, while the UK Law Officers would insist on our sending out a small army of inspectors to do so forthwith.

On only one occasion were we able to engage in the kind of behaviour practised by some of our counterparts. When the French police failed to prevent their farmers blocking ports and roads to obstruct the imports of British lamb, we banned imports of French poultry for a while because, supposedly, of an outbreak there of an obscure malady called Newcastle disease. When my French colleague and very good friend Guy Legras rang me to ask, 'What is this Newcastle disease?', I explained that it was a disease that prevented French chickens getting to Newcastle. The lamb blockade was lifted and normal service resumed.

To my amazement, this was the point at which we received a notification of the Commission's intention to regulate the British sausage. As they pointed out (correctly), British pork sausages frequently contained less than 50 per cent pork. The Commission proposed to remedy this. We felt obliged to explain to them that, unfortunately, their plan coincided with Jim Hacker in *Yes, Minister* becoming Prime Minister – by defending the British sausage! A video of the programme was despatched to Brussels and the British sausage was saved.

* * *

The Prime Minister reserved her particular distrust for the world-weary and wily Italian Foreign Minister Andreotti, whom she regarded as slippery and unreliable. In one exchange with him on some quasi-scientific subject, she reminded him that she was a chemist. I asked my Italian colleague what Andreotti had muttered as he turned away. This turned out to be that he would never buy a prescription from her: 'I would be afraid that she might poison me.'

Andreotti, meanwhile, was preparing an ambush in Milan. He proposed that there should be an inter-governmental conference to amend the European treaties. When the Prime Minister opposed this, she was outvoted nine to one. While treaty change required unanimity, the procedural decision did not.

Margaret Thatcher returned to the delegation room. As she walked out to meet the press, I asked her not to say that she would never agree to treaty change. It was just possible that we might be able to negotiate some changes that would be acceptable to us.

She swept off with no reply. But under intense pressure from the journalists, she did not say that she would never agree to any treaty change – only that she was not convinced of the need for it.

On our return to London, Michael Butler, David Williamson and I sought and were granted a licence to explore with the other member states treaty changes acceptable to us. 'Yes,' was the reply, 'but please bear in mind that when you come back, I may disavow you.'

Michael Butler and his successor, David Hannay, negotiated with exceptional skill in Brussels. David Hannay was especially adept at influencing ministers despite, or perhaps because of, the fact that he bore an uncanny resemblance to Sir Humphrey Appleby in *Yes, Minister* and sometimes sounded like him too.

Williamson and I sought, once again, to reach an understanding with the French, who at the time had no more desire than we did to see a large extension of the powers of the Commission or the European Parliament.

My French counterpart, Pierre de Boissieu, great-nephew of General de Gaulle, was adamant on this point. When Thatcher told Mitterrand that she could accept the Boissieu plan for the European Parliament, Mitterrand was delighted. 'But what is the Boissieu plan?' he enquired.

By the time of the Luxembourg European Council in December 1985, we had reached agreement on the draft of a new treaty which incorporated measures to speed up decision-making on the single market. But the other member states also wanted commitments to an eventual monetary union and the abolition of frontier controls. Neither issue was negotiable for us and, on her arrival in Luxembourg, I gave Mrs Thatcher a list of twelve points we had to win to render the text acceptable to us.

This had the advantage of channelling her energies in a positive direction and, after two days, and at the cost of driving the others to distraction, she had won eleven of them.

The outstanding issue was the determination of the Ministry of Agriculture to maintain our ability to prevent the import of animals and plants from other countries, come what may. By the time they had spent three hours debating this, the other heads of government had heard more than enough about our anti-rabies regime. As the discussion had reached complete deadlock, I fed into the meeting a new formula, devised by my deputy in London, Stephen Wall, that did enable us to maintain our controls.

A relieved Geoffrey Howe read this out to the meeting. As the Luxembourg Prime Minister went around the table, Kohl, Mitterrand and the others all accepted – until he got to Mrs Thatcher, who rejected it! The others by now did not know whether to laugh or cry. A short break in the proceedings enabled us to persuade a reluctant Prime Minister to go along with our own proposal.

We had no more talented defender than Stephen Wall of British interests in Europe in many subsequent negotiations, described in his memoir *A Stranger in Europe*.

Margaret Thatcher subsequently gave the impression of regretting it. But, at the time, she was very pleased at the outcome in Luxembourg. We had succeeded in obliging the others to negotiate to a large extent on terrain of our own choosing – the completion of the single market.

Amidst the myriad respects in which the EU is criticised, often with good reason, today, it frequently is forgotten that the accession negotiations in which we were involved at the time were important in helping Greece, Spain and Portugal to consolidate their newly established democracies. In more recent times, the ability to join the EU was extremely important to the countries of eastern Europe as they escaped from the clutches of the Comintern.

No one who witnessed Helmut Kohl and, in due course, Jacques Chirac, bellowing and thumping the table in support of German and French farmers could reasonably accuse her of having been overzealous in defence of British interests. She still felt, at this stage, that with enlargement and the drive to complete the single market, the Community was developing in a direction compatible with our interests. Institutionally, the Foreign Office had a near-pathological fear of being left out of European integration. Yet there were obvious advantages in being 'left out' of the Schengen Agreement abolishing frontier controls.

CHAPTER XIV

DEFYING ADAM SMITH

Throughout this period, an increasingly intense discussion was being conducted between the Treasury, the Foreign Office and 10 Downing Street about the European Exchange Rate Mechanism (ERM). The Foreign Office institutionally was in favour of Britain joining, on foreign policy grounds. Geoffrey Howe, on becoming Foreign Secretary, had been converted to this point of view.

The Treasury initially had been sceptical. To my amusement, however, on arriving in my office one Monday morning, I was informed that overnight, or at any rate over the weekend, they had undergone a Damascene conversion. This was because they had lost confidence in the monetary aggregates – M0, measuring essentially cash, and M3, measuring wider credit – control of which had been supposed to be the key to containing inflation.

When the Prime Minister asked Peter Middleton,

head of the Treasury, why they now favoured joining the ERM, he said it was because she would not be there one day. Joining the ERM would reinforce discipline against inflation.

I was an admirer of Nigel Lawson, who was never afraid to stand up to the Prime Minister. The Confederation of British Industry, the *Financial Times* et al. were in favour of joining. But within the Foreign Office at the time, I was a solitary sceptic, apart from one of the economic advisers, who agreed with me. I could not believe that we had forgotten so quickly the damage inflicted on the British economy by the failed attempts to maintain a fixed exchange rate against the dollar, the resultant fiasco for the Wilson government and the similar debacle when Edward Heath took Britain into the European monetary 'snake', precursor of the ERM, from which we had to withdraw within a matter of weeks. In my humble and in this period very old-fashioned opinion, in determining currency values, it was impossible to do a better job than the market.

I was reinforced in this opinion by Eddie George, future Governor of the Bank of England, far more of a sceptic than the then Governor, Robin Leigh-Pemberton.

On three occasions in 1985 Nigel Lawson tried and failed to persuade the Prime Minister of the advantages of joining. In one of his letters he acknowledged that, if we joined, sterling would come under pressure in an election, because of fears that Labour might win. Therefore, in an election period, we would need to take a holiday from the ERM!

But he was firmly opposed to European monetary union. In the run-up to the European Council in Luxembourg in June 1985, he warned against any new commitment to monetary union, with which Margaret Thatcher of course agreed. 'Economic and monetary union', however, had been an official EC objective since the days of Edward Heath.

Her refusal to have Britain join the ERM led subsequently to the departures from her government of Geoffrey Howe and Nigel Lawson. Sterling, meanwhile, had been fluctuating widely against the deutschmark. When we did join the ERM in October 1990, I telephoned Charles Powell in No. 10 to ask why on earth we had done so. He replied that the government by then had run out of any other ideas as to what to do.

CHAPTER XV

'IF YOU WANT TO GET OUT OF A HOLE, THE FIRST THING TO DO IS TO STOP DIGGING'

In August 1987, I was despatched by the Prime Minister to be the British Ambassador in South Africa. She found it intensely frustrating that, despite having several hundred thousand British citizens and dual nationals in South Africa and being by far the biggest investors there, we had so little influence.

In her meeting with the singularly unpleasant President P. W. Botha in June 1984, she had urged him to release Nelson Mandela, who had spent twenty years in prison, and to engage in negotiations on a new constitution, to no avail. Botha had initiated some reforms, but these were designed to modernise apartheid, not to abolish it. A pro-German sympathiser during the war, he had no love for the British, his mother having been interned by us during the Boer War.

Meanwhile, Margaret Thatcher was under pressure from the rest of the Commonwealth to impose ever more extensive sanctions against South Africa, running contrary to her desire not to isolate the country and to preserve our economic interests. She wanted us to play a more active role than the Foreign Office had been ready to contemplate, damage limitation being the prevailing mantra. The embassy was accused of a belief in 'keeping our heads down' and better-nottery.

On arrival in Cape Town, my first action was to seek out Helen Suzman, who had opposed apartheid in the South African Parliament on her own for thirteen years. I found this lady that I so admired to be not only the best guide to South African politics, but the best company to be found there too. Knowing that her opinions horrified the majority of the white population, she declared, 'Like everyone else, I long to be loved – but I am not prepared to make any concessions whatsoever!' When the then Prime Minister, John Vorster, declared that he could not see anything wrong with apartheid, she suggested that he should try visiting a township, 'heavily disguised as a human being'.

With this very striking exception, I was convinced that the South African political drama was going to be played out between the Afrikaners and the leaders of the black population and that I must avoid falling into the easy trap of consorting mainly with the liberal English speakers who agreed with us anyway.

Over the next few months, I sought to form friendships with Ton Vosloo, head of the main Afrikaans press group; Johan Heyns, head of the Dutch Reformed Church, who had declared apartheid a heresy; Gerhard de Kock, head of the Reserve Bank; and Pieter de Lange, head of the secretive Afrikaner society the Broederbond, who, I found, had circulated to its members a remarkable paper arguing that 'the greatest risk is not taking any risks'. I met several younger *verligte* (enlightened) National Party MPs who understood that the politics of repression could not succeed over time.

I also met the supposedly very conservative head of the National Party in the Transvaal, F. W. de Klerk, who, noting that I had been at Lancaster House, said that, if he had his way, South Africa would not make the mistake the Rhodesians had.

What was that? I enquired. 'Leaving it much too late to negotiate with the real black leaders,' was the reply.

The country at the time was in the grip of severe repression, with thousands of people in detention without trial and the murder of activists by agents of military intelligence and the police security branch. The ANC and other organisations were banned, their leaders in prison or in exile. P. W. Botha had established a militaristic regime in which total reliance was placed on the security forces, who were encouraged to act with no holds barred. When I asked General Johan van der Merwe, head of the security police, why the country was relatively quiet, his reply was, 'This time we have locked up all the right people!' As he went on to explain that black South Africans lacked organisational skills, I asked how it was then that they had managed not long before to arrange a demonstration of 100,000 people outside Port Elizabeth.

In my first encounter with P. W. Botha, with the Prime Minister's strong approval, I delivered a clear warning about the consequences of further major cross-border raids of the kind that had sabotaged the attempted Commonwealth negotiating mission in 1986. This was a message I also delivered to his principal henchman, the Defence Minister, Magnus Malan.

Not long after my arrival, P. W. Botha intensified the repression by banning the United Democratic Front, which had been organising mass demonstrations and represented, in effect, the internal wing of the ANC. I decided that it was time to deliver a decidedly undiplomatic speech in Johannesburg, declaring that repression could not solve South Africa's problems. The apartheid laws must be repealed and Mandela released. 'If you want to get out of a hole, the first thing to do is to stop digging.'

This was splashed all over the South African press, including in *Beeld* and *Die Burger*, where the editors, Wim Wepener and Ebbe Dommisse respectively, both agreed with it. At dinner that evening with the Afrikaner entrepreneur and critic of apartheid Johann Rupert and me, De Klerk told us that he had not been consulted about the ban and would have done things very differently. The exuberant Foreign Minister, Pik Botha, protested strongly about the speech, before telling me that he agreed with it. Nelson Mandela, still in prison, turned out to have read it too.

Pik Botha asked me to see the President again to try to calm him down. The 'Groot Krokodil', as he was unaffectionately known, even by his colleagues, was in his usual truculent form. He had made reforms, but the west had let him down. With their sanctions, the US had lost all influence. Mandela could not be released unless he renounced violence. Otherwise he would have to be arrested again the next day.

I said that if Mandela died in jail, that would have catastrophic consequences. We did not believe in isolating South Africa, but could not stop them isolating themselves.

A few days later, I was back, to argue, as the recording tapes whirred away, for the lives of the Sharpeville Six, condemned to death for having murdered a township deputy mayor. All their appeals having failed, they were within forty-eight hours of being executed.

P. W. Botha would meet me in his darkened study, with only a green desk lamp offering any light, his dark glasses and domed forehead giving an eerie impression, conjuring up images of what it must have been like meeting the Führer in his bunker. I had arranged with my friend Johan Heyns, head of the Reformed Church, that we would both see P. W. Botha about the Sharpeville Six on the same day. Very much against his wishes, on this occasion Botha gave way.

I tried also to form friendships with a number of ex-Robben Islanders who had served long sentences with Mandela, including Neville Alexander and Fikile Bam, who had appeared in the film *Robben Island Our University*, and Dikgang Moseneke, who went on to become Deputy Chief Justice. In Soweto I befriended Albertina Sisulu, wife of Mandela's closest colleague and fellow prisoner, Walter Sisulu. I turned up in court to show support for the Delmas treason triallists, Popo Molefe and Terror Lekota, who were on trial for their lives. I established regular contact with Cyril Ramaphosa, the impressive young head of the National Union of Mineworkers.

I started to give parties at the embassy to which I invited some former Robben Islanders together with some of the *verligte* Nationalists, without telling either side who else would be coming.

Archbishop Desmond Tutu had boycotted my predecessor because of Thatcher's opposition to further sanctions. But I had enlisted the help of Robert Runcie, Archbishop of Canterbury, to tell him that, in view of my role in Rhodesia, I could hardly be considered a supporter of apartheid.

As Desmond Tutu, who I whole-heartedly admired, observed to me and others, 'When the Dutch and British settlers arrived in South Africa, they had bibles and we had the land. After a while, we found that they had the land and we had the bibles!'

My meetings with him always opened with the words 'Let us pray!' And he was absolutely right: there was plenty to pray about at the time. When I got to know him better, I suggested that this was a way of reminding me that there were three of us in the room – and I was outnumbered. We never did agree about the pros and cons of general sanctions that would have put hundreds of thousands of farm workers out of work and brought down the neighbouring countries long before South Africa, but he accepted the role we could play in helping to get Mandela released and supported our efforts in the townships.

As P. W. Botha continued to pursue policies with no regard to the economic consequences for South Africa, I sought help from the leading Afrikaner entrepreneur and truly statesmanlike figure Anton Rupert. Over lunch in

Stellenbosch, he explained to me that he had no influence with his President whatsoever. Realising that I would find this hard to understand, he showed me a translated summary of an exchange with Botha, in which he had urged him, very politely but firmly, to avoid actions that could contribute to the further isolation of South Africa. The President's response was to tell him to mind his own business. Fortunately for South Africa, F. W. de Klerk's approach was to listen very carefully to the advice he received from the Ruperts and other leaders of the business community.

* * *

Visits to Soweto in this fraught period were a lot of fun. The vast sprawling township, home to a million people, was territory unknown to all but a handful of white South Africans. Amidst the tens of thousands of tiny two-roomed 'matchbox' houses, in one of which I used to meet Mandela, there were enclaves of greater prosperity, one of them housing a riding school and a bowling green. The main night-club was housed in a basement under the police station.

The owner of the immensely popular magazine *Drum*, my friend Jim Bailey, son of a wealthy Randlord and a Hurricane pilot during the war, hired progressive editors, including at one point Anthony Sampson, but had to keep reminding them that Sowetans were interested in their political rights, but also in girls, jazz and football, and for women, beautification, from which the current reforming Mayor of Johannesburg, Herman Mashaba, had started making a fortune.

An exceptionally popular figure in the township was Gary Bailey, former goalkeeper of Manchester United, then playing with the Kaizer Chiefs. Local derbies against the Orlando Pirates were marked by the presence of witchdoctors with strange objects behind the goals, with a view to keeping the ball out of the net. The Sowetans did not take this mumbo-jumbo too seriously, save as a spectacle to be enjoyed.

As well as the magnificent choir in the Anglican cathedral, Soweto was a breeding ground for talented musicians. To enliven sedate parties in Pretoria, we would import jazz bands from Soweto, who performed like demons and have become deservedly well known today.

The largest circulation newspaper in South Africa, *The Sowetan*, was in the hands of a remarkable editor, Aggrey Klaaste, who, coming from the Black Consciousness tradition, was determined to prove himself as independent of the ANC as he was of the regime. I arranged for him an interview in London with Margaret Thatcher. The editorial staff in the newsroom worked with ancient typewriters and green eyeshades, in conscious imitation of Hollywood movies in the '30s.

The Sowetans were and are tough, resourceful, humorous and entrepreneurial. As in other townships, they needed help with the very small amounts of capital required to get small businesses started – garages, brick-making kilns, carpentry and sewing cooperatives to make the uniforms in which even the poorest families tried to send their children to school. They reserved some biting humour for self-promoting visitors like Jesse Jackson and 'consciousness-raising' concerts abroad, whose proceeds never seemed to get as far as them.

The uncrowned king of Gugulethu, which housed 70,000 people outside Cape Town, was a Catholic priest, Father Basil van Rensburg. As a priest in District Six, Father Basil, holding a crucifix in front of him, had prevented the bulldozer drivers from touching his church or the nearby mosque, when every other building in the settlement was razed to the ground.

Visiting one of his church services was an experience not to be missed, as the congregation, however impoverished, appeared with all their children and everyone else in their Sunday best, with the priest in his ceremonial finery, the massed choirs bursting into song and the sound of a hundred marimbas creating an electric atmosphere.

Other priests helped with our projects in Crossroads and in Mamelodi outside Pretoria, where Dr Ribeiro was murdered by agents of the regime. In Alexandra, another area of unrest, on the edge of Johannesburg, we tried to protect from closure and help with funding the clinic run by Dr Francis Wilson, accused of treating demonstrators hurt in clashes with the police. My wife supported Operation Hunger in the rural areas, the anti-apartheid women's movement, the Black Sash, and organisations to help street children in Pretoria and Cape Town.

Venturing into these areas was not without risk, but our friends in the townships would forewarn us whenever they believed there was a risk of violence. We ended up supporting 300 township projects, with funding provided first by Chris Patten, then by Lynda Chalker, as the Ministers for Overseas Development. Of invaluable help in these efforts were our consular staff – John Doble and Roy Reeve in Johannesburg, Mick Frost in Cape Town – and, within the embassy, John Sawers, who went on to serve as the British Ambassador to the United Nations, then as head of the Secret Intelligence Service.

The government were determined to suppress their main thorn in the press at the time, the *Weekly Mail* under Anton Harber. When they banned it for long enough, they hoped, to put it out of business before the courts could overturn the banning order, I took the embassy Rolls-Royce to the newspaper office and handed over enough funding to ensure it could survive.

CHAPTER XVI

'THE WHOLE WORLD WILL BE AGAINST YOU'

The Prime Minister continued to bombard P. W. Botha with messages demanding the release of Nelson Mandela and repeal of the apartheid laws, to no avail. I told her that we should concentrate on seeking to help achieve independence for Namibia.

This wild and beautiful territory had been controlled by South Africa ever since the Germans were ousted in World War I. In the capital, Windhoek, the two main streets still were entitled Kaiser Wilhelm Strasse and Goering Strasse (after Hermann Goering's father, who had served as the first Governor there, presiding over a bloody repression of the Herero uprising).

The South West African People's Organisation (SWAPO) were conducting attempted guerrilla operations from across the border in Angola. In response, the South Africans were in the habit of regarding southern

Angola as a free-fire zone. Tens of thousands of Cuban troops by this time were present in Angola, supported by the Russians. For the Reagan administration, my friend Chester Crocker was trying to broker a settlement based on the South Africans withdrawing from Namibia and the Cubans from Angola.

In a classic demonstration of the knots diplomats can tie themselves into, this 'linkage' was rejected by the Europeans, including the Foreign Office, as, in their view, the South Africans should withdraw whatever the Cubans did. This was entirely self-defeating, as the South Africans weren't going to withdraw unless the Cubans did too, and it was desirable to get them out of Angola anyway. I told Crocker that, whatever his British counterparts might say, the Prime Minister agreed with him.

In October 1987, the Angolan government and the Cuban military launched a major offensive intended finally to crush Jonas Savimbi's rebel UNITA movement and their South African allies. They were ambushed on the Lomba River by the South Africans, who then overreached themselves by pursuing their opponents back to their base at Cuito Cuanavale, where they were halted by Cuban heavy armour.

In Windhoek, I was briefed by a half-mad South African colonel on these battles. He contended that victory for South Africa in Namibia was certain – but for the efforts of the enemy within. When I enquired who the enemy within were, he replied, 'The churches, the trade unions and the teachers.'

The South African Foreign Minister, Pik Botha, for the past fifteen years had been one of the most colourful figures on the international scene. Built like a buffalo, he would sit in his shirtsleeves, a thick black lock of hair falling across his face, complaining about the world's supposed injustices towards South Africa.

Sessions with him were always entertaining, but never short. Over a bottle of whisky on the table between us, he would tell me, with great solemnity, that not a single South African soldier was present in Namibia. Whereupon we would both burst out laughing, as several people I knew were serving there.

Never hesitating to perjure himself in public, he was devastatingly frank in private, not least about his colleagues. Whatever his faults, which were not small ones, I always found him an ally in arguing with his President for a Namibia settlement and internal reform.

Pik Botha kept telling me that he was arguing for a change in South African policy, as was his Director General, Neil van Heerden, one of the ablest and most dedicated public servants I had ever met anywhere. Pik had been saying this for years. But this time I believed him – if the Cubans could be persuaded to withdraw.

For the war by this time had become intensely unpopular in Cuba, with plenty of casualties and limited results. But I knew from my Afrikaner contacts that it was becoming increasingly unpopular with them too. Many of those serving in Angola were conscripts. Their families were worried about them. Johan Heyns enquired publicly why young South Africans were being asked to defend their country 200 miles inside Angola.

The Russians, increasingly disillusioned, were beginning to contemplate cutting their losses in Africa. Gorbachev's Foreign Minister, Eduard Shevardnadze, caused consternation by telling the Soviet Union's African allies that, in future, relations with them were going to be conducted on the basis of cost–benefit analysis! I started receiving notes from Boris Asoyan, the de facto Soviet envoy in southern Africa, approving of my public statements that what South Africa needed was not more sanctions or armed struggle, but a negotiated outcome.

In May 1988, we made available a venue in London for the first in a new round of negotiations between the South Africans, Cubans and Angolans. Further meetings followed at different venues, all of them prepared with help from our Ambassador in Angola, James Glaze, as the Americans had no embassy there. We also had to do a good deal of the heavy lifting in support of Pik Botha and Neil van Heerden in Pretoria. On 9 May, the Prime Minister wrote to P. W. Botha that 'it would be a major prize to secure the withdrawal of Cuban troops from Angola and an internationally accepted settlement in Namibia'.

Stung by their reverse on the Lomba River, the Cubans at last had come up with a militarily effective response, moving their heavy tanks much closer to the Namibian border. Military sanctions had limited the South Africans' ability to acquire heavy tanks and modernise their front-line aircraft. As a Cuban column approached the hydro-electric power station on the border, they were attacked by the South Africans, who inflicted heavy casualties. In retaliation, the Cubans bombed the dam, which the South Africans controlled, killing eleven of them. Having tasted blood, some of it their own, both sides drew back from further exploits of this kind.

In August 1988, the Cubans formally accepted the linkage between the withdrawal of their forces from Angola and Namibian independence. By November, a schedule had been worked out whereby the Cuban forces would withdraw from southern Angola and then leave. In December, the agreement was signed, a triumph of persistence for Chester Crocker and his team.

By now, the Reagan administration was giving way to that of George H. W. Bush and, to my dismay, Crocker was not reappointed. Crocker told me that we were going to have to take on much of the burden of assuring that the agreement was in fact implemented. It had opened the way for a ceasefire to come into effect in Namibia on 1 April 1989, to be followed by elections under UN control.

*   *   *

In March, Margaret Thatcher was due to make an African tour, ending in Malawi. To show support for the UN plan and our military helping to implement it, I wanted her to appear in Namibia on the first day of the ceasefire. The Foreign Office had reasons to fear that this was far too risky. As usual, she took pleasure in overruling them.

It was agreed that I would have to recommend from Windhoek whether the risk was worth taking. The UN Special Representative, Martti Ahtisaari, and the UN military commander, General Prem Chand, both wanted her to come. The press on her plane were told only after take-off from Malawi that they were headed for Namibia, not Heathrow.

So, as Namibia fell under UN control, the prime ministerial VC10 arrived at Windhoek airport. Mrs Thatcher had lunch in their tented camp with the British military contingent. The rest of us had fizzy water, but I had asked the military to provide Denis Thatcher with an otherwise indistinguishable gin and tonic, earning a huge grin from him. We set off to visit the main British investment in

Namibia, the Rössing uranium mine, where Rio Tinto had set an example in terms of housing, health, safety and pensions far superior to those anywhere else in the territory.

By the time we returned to Windhoek, there were reports of large-scale crossings of the border by armed SWAPO forces in contravention of the ceasefire, accompanied by violent clashes. The SWAPO forces were supposed not to cross the border with their weapons, while the South African military were confined to their bases. Both sides were behaving as if the ceasefire agreement were no longer in place.

In a critical meeting with the UN Representative, Martti Ahtisaari, later to become President of Finland, Thatcher said that she would oppose any South African withdrawal from the agreement but, to save it, he would need to get the UN Secretary General, Javier Pérez de Cuéllar, to authorise South African ground forces to stop the armed SWAPO incursions.

The scene shifted to a long and extremely difficult meeting with Pik Botha at the airport. Under pressure from the military in Pretoria, he was adamant that the South Africans would have to call in air strikes against the SWAPO columns. Thatcher told him that if they did so, 'The whole world will be against you – led by me!'

This went on for two hours until, mercifully, Denis Thatcher intervened, as the Prime Minister had to catch her plane. As I returned to Windhoek, I was told that, in a display of political courage by them, Pérez de Cuéllar and Ahtisaari had accepted the need for action to deal with the incursions, and Pik Botha told me that the air strikes had been called off.

Margaret Thatcher boarded her plane reluctantly. She clearly was attracted by continuing to conduct the affairs of Namibia. She had some justification for claiming in her memoirs that she had been 'in the right place, at the right time'.

Meeting the SWAPO leaders on their return to Windhoek, I told them that I did not expect them to feel much empathy for a Conservative British government, or vice versa. We hoped they would rethink their Marxist economic views (which, to a large extent, they did). But we were determined to see that they got a fair chance in the elections, which I expected them to win. If they did, we would help them in government.

Shortly afterwards, a friend of mine in SWAPO, the leading white member of the party, Anton Lubowski, was assassinated. I attended his funeral in the township outside Windhoek, at which the SWAPO leaders made an emotional plea for calm. I had no doubt who was responsible for this killing. It later was proved to have been a member of the Magnus Malan-sponsored death squad, the so-called Civil Cooperation Bureau.

This was not the end of this saga. As the Namibian elections, due at the end of November, approached, I was sure that we would witness another attempt by South African military intelligence to disrupt them. The only question was what form this would take.

In Pretoria I suddenly was summoned, with the other western Ambassadors, to a meeting with Pik Botha and General Jannie Geldenhuys, head of the South African Defence Force. Pik read out intercepted radio messages purporting to show that another massive SWAPO incursion was planned, with the connivance of the Kenyan contingent in the UN military force.

As we controlled the UN communications in Namibia, it took me less than three hours to ascertain, and to warn Van Heerden, that these messages were fake. A furious Pik Botha had been misled by his own intelligence services. As usual, no action appeared to be taken against those responsible for this deception.

The crisis passed, with SWAPO winning the election by a large majority. Attending the independence celebrations, there was no doubting the sense of joy, and also of relief, amidst the vast crowd at the attainment of self-rule and the end of a bitter and bloody conflict.

CHAPTER XVII

A FRIENDSHIP WITH DE KLERK

In January 1989, on the eve of the new parliamentary session, P. W. Botha had suffered a stroke. My betting had always been on F. W. de Klerk to succeed him. In February, De Klerk was elected the new head of the National Party, narrowly defeating the ostensibly more *verligte* Finance Minister, Barend du Plessis. I was glad at the outcome, as I had been impressed by De Klerk's strength of character, which was going to be badly needed in the months ahead. I also believed that it was easier for hawks than for doves to make peace, once they have decided to do so. But P. W. Botha was determined to cling on as President.

At the opening of Parliament, De Klerk had asked Helen Suzman why everyone thought he was *verkramp* (reactionary). Because you never make a *verligte* speech, was the reply. De Klerk now proceeded to make a very *verligte* speech indeed, promising full civil rights to all

South Africans and a democratic system from which no community would be excluded.

In a meeting with De Klerk at this time, I passed on an invitation to meet the Prime Minister. He said that he regarded the ties with Britain as the most important relationship South Africa currently had, as the US administration was hamstrung by Congress.

Following Chet Crocker's departure, I found myself operating on a pitch with no sign of the Americans anywhere on it. Congress having enacted comprehensive sanctions, the administration was unable to give any encouragement to De Klerk. Crocker's successor observed to the Secretary of State, James Baker, that they had written themselves out of the story 'just when it was getting interesting'.

I yield to no one in my admiration for George Bush Sr and James Baker. But with good reason they were totally preoccupied with diplomacy in relation to the break-up of the Soviet Union. South Africa barely figures in either of their memoirs.

De Klerk said that he realised that we wanted to see a new impetus for change. I said that if he was able to take South Africa in a new direction, he would get our active support. But if the security police and military intelligence were allowed to continue their present activities, including murder squads, unchecked, there was no way any of us were going to be able to help South Africa. I gave him the names of a brigadier and a colonel in military intelligence who, despite all the denials, were continuing to supply arms and ammunition to the rebel RENAMO movement in Mozambique.

De Klerk told me that he heard what I was saying. He had never been involved in authorising these activities and was determined to deal with them. But, he added carefully, as I would understand, he would have to deal with the security forces with a velvet glove.

De Klerk's friends were not the securocrats beloved of P. W. Botha but the Johannesburg business community, and precisely those Afrikaners, including the Rupert family, who had been at loggerheads with P. W. Botha. De Klerk understood that without turning the capital outflow into investment capital inflows, South Africa had no hope of achieving rates of growth higher than the population increase, a concept the security force leaders had never bothered to try to understand.

De Klerk, who belonged to the Dopper faction of the Dutch Reformed Church in the hyper-conservative university city of Potchefstroom, also took his religion seriously. (When dancing was banned on the campus in Potchefstroom, the students' union enquired if sex was also banned. The students concluded that it was – as it could lead to dancing!)

Following the assassination of Dulcie September, the

ANC representative in Paris, I was asked to give P. W. Botha's entourage a fierce warning as to what would happen if any such attack were mounted against the ANC in London. We knew that an attack was being planned. It had better be called off immediately.

As my friend Kobus Meiring had been appointed Administrator of the Cape, I asked him to promise that the magnificent beaches would be opened forthwith to people of all races, which he needed little encouragement to do, having told me how embarrassed he was that his own holiday apartment had on the beach in front of it a 'Whites Only' sign.

In May 1989, I had another meeting with De Klerk about his reform plans. After the whites-only elections, scheduled for September, in which he faced a strong challenge from the right-wing Afrikaner Conservative Party, led by Andries Treurnicht, he planned negotiations on a new constitution. I told him that we remained extremely concerned about the activities of the lunatic fringes of the security establishment, which we knew were not authorised by him. He said again that any South African President had to retain the support of the army and the police. But he was determined to assert civilian control over the military.

I saw P. W. Botha, mainly to reassure myself that he was not going to be able to stage a comeback. Tired and fragile, he clearly was in no condition to carry on much longer, though I doubted that he would go gracefully. I felt a sense of great relief and satisfaction at seeing the last of him. This was a man who never should have been put in charge of the fortunes of his or any other country. For he it was who had personally authorised his physician to experiment with chemical and biological weapons for use against enemies of the regime.

CHAPTER XVIII

'YOU CAN TELL YOUR PRIME MINISTER THAT SHE WILL NOT BE DISAPPOINTED'

The next step was to arrange for F. W. De Klerk to meet Mrs Thatcher at Chequers. This was still an unpopular thing to do. But she impressed on De Klerk, with her customary lack of ambiguity, the need to carry through the Namibia settlement and to release Nelson Mandela. She found De Klerk open-minded and a refreshing change from P. W. Botha, but his replies enigmatic. He had an election to fight against the Afrikaner *bittereinders*. As we stood on the steps of Chequers watching De Klerk's motorcade depart, she told me that she still was uncertain how far he would be prepared to go. I said that I believed De Klerk would go further than she imagined.

There were still many who doubted whether De Klerk's

reformist language was anything more than a change of style. His brother Wimpie, who was playing a leading role in the discussions of Afrikaner academics with the ANC, told me that he feared his brother was far too conservative to be a good President. I told him that he must know his brother better than I did, but I thought De Klerk would prove him wrong.

P. W. Botha invited Mandela to tea with him in his office in Cape Town. Mandela's warder helped him to knot his tie; he had not had much use for one in prison. Niel Barnard, head of the National Intelligence Service, knelt down to tie Mandela's shoelaces. The meeting was courteous. The Justice Minister, Kobie Coetsee, and Barnard had advised Mandela against raising contentious issues with the President. So they talked about South African history. The meeting lasted less than half an hour. At the end, Mandela asked Botha to release all political prisoners. Botha said that he could not do that.

Mandela was generous about this meeting in his memoirs. What it really amounted to was an attempt by P. W. Botha to upstage De Klerk and to show that politically he was not dead yet.

It did not take much longer for matters to come to a head with P. W. Botha. He reacted furiously to an announcement that De Klerk would be meeting President Kaunda of Zambia. De Klerk and the Cabinet asked him to retire gracefully, which he declined to do, berating his colleagues and displaying, in De Klerk's words, his 'irascible and cantankerous nature'. They insisted unanimously on his immediate resignation, with De Klerk taking over as President.

In the elections, the National Party won ninety-three of the seats in Parliament, giving them a clear majority, but the Conservative Party won 40 per cent of the Afrikaner votes. On election day, a number of coloured youths were killed in clashes with the police in the Cape townships. Archbishop Tutu called for a protest march in Cape Town on 13 September.

Tutu asked me to see him at his home in Bishopscourt, where he gave me a message to the Prime Minister, asking for her help in getting the march permitted. From Bishopscourt I went to see Pik Botha and Neil van Heerden, who needed no convincing that the march should be permitted, but the security chiefs, as usual, were opposed.

Next morning, Johan Heyns walked into my office, with several other leaders of the Dutch Reformed Church, having heard that we were trying to get the demonstration allowed, as they were themselves. They went off to see De Klerk, who overruled the security chiefs to permit the demonstration. I was asked to get assurances from the church leaders that, if the police stood on the sidelines, they would help to ensure that the demonstration was peaceful. When it took place, we held our breath as a huge crowd assembled. The church and UDF leaders marshalled it effectively, with no violence.

The Peace March, as it became known, marked a turning point in South Africa's history, as De Klerk went on to authorise demonstrations in other major cities. The Prime Minister congratulated De Klerk, but emphasised the need to release Mandela and Walter Sisulu. I told Desmond Tutu that we were working on all the issues of concern to him.

The Justice Minister, Kobie Coetsee, even under P. W. Botha had tried to enlist my help to get Mandela released. At De Klerk's inauguration, he rushed up to ask me if he was going to announce the release of Mandela. I said that De Klerk had told me that Mandela's release would require preparation and he would never take such a decision without involving his ministers.

I saw De Klerk in his office in the Union Buildings on the following day. He commented that his talk with Mrs Thatcher at Chequers had been tougher than those with Kohl and the other European leaders, because she had talked to him more bluntly. I was glad to find that, far from being alarmed at the advance of the Conservative Party, De Klerk had reached the opposite conclusion, namely that 70 per cent of the white electorate had voted for reform.

In October, I pressed Van Heerden about the need to

demonstrate that all this *glasnost* (openness) was not just words. I pressed for the release of Walter Sisulu and the other long-term Robben Islanders. He promised that Pik Botha was ready for a fight over this with General Malan and the police. Thatcher's influence was important. He added that the Namibia agreement would never have been achieved without our efforts and those of Chet Crocker (his own contribution having been second to none).

I said that De Klerk wanted to create a climate in which Mandela could be released and negotiations could take place. This would be the vital next step in doing so.

On the evening of 10 October, De Klerk telephoned Mrs Thatcher to tell her that he was about to announce the release of Walter Sisulu, Ahmed Kathrada, Andrew Mlangeni and five other companions of Mandela on Robben Island.

There followed a major fracas at the Commonwealth Conference in Kuala Lumpur, which the Prime Minister enjoyed rather more than her Foreign Secretary, John Major. As no one else was prepared to acknowledge these major advances by De Klerk, instead wanting to intensify sanctions against him, she did so in a statement of her own. The British press had a field day, contending that she was isolated, as indeed she was. Given that within four months De Klerk was to announce the release of Mandela, her stand and the statement she issued made a great deal more sense than theirs did.

Invited by Albertina Sisulu to the homecoming in Soweto for her husband and his colleagues, it was a very emotional moment to see these venerable gentlemen, clad in cardigans or waistcoats, legendary figures in the history of the ANC, none of them looking much like revolutionaries, though most were members of the South African Communist Party.

I told them that I had spoken to the government about not interfering with the rally to welcome them back to Soweto. We would be doing everything we could to help get Mandela released in the New Year. That would depend on the demonstrations remaining peaceful. Walter Sisulu said that he would be seeking to ensure this.

The government were continuing to talk about the need to protect group rights, conceived of as a way to help safeguard Afrikaner interests. I urged on De Klerk's deputy, the scholarly Gerrit Viljoen, the need to change the language, and to talk about minority rights, which did not have the same connotations of privilege.

The destruction of the Berlin Wall began on 9 November. De Klerk had grasped the full significance of the impending collapse of the Soviet Union, discrediting the securocrat doctrine of the Communist-inspired 'total onslaught'. I confirmed to him that the Russians, who, anyway, had not been very impressed by the achievements of the armed struggle, except as 'armed propaganda', were urging the ANC to negotiate.

Mandela conveyed his thanks to De Klerk for the release of his comrades. He had observed the authorisation of demonstrations that would have been banned, the opening up of the beaches and planned repeal of more apartheid legislation, concluding that there was indeed a new hand on the tiller. He wrote to De Klerk, as he had to P. W. Botha, urging talks between the government and the ANC, but reiterating that the ANC would not accept any preconditions, especially not suspension of the armed struggle.

On 13 December, Mandela met De Klerk in the same office in Cape Town as he had P. W. Botha. De Klerk 'listened to what I had to say. This was a novel experience,' observed Mandela, who said that the concept of 'group rights' was seen by his people as a way to preserve apartheid. 'We will have to change it then,' said De Klerk.

*   *   *

In January 1990, I returned to London to discuss with the Prime Minister and the Foreign Secretary, Douglas Hurd, what we should do if De Klerk released Mandela and opened the way for negotiations with the ANC. They agreed that we should lift the voluntary ban on new investment, Hurd would visit South Africa at the time of the Namibia independence celebrations and we should intensify our efforts to get South Africa to sign the Nuclear Non-Proliferation Treaty.

I heard that De Klerk had made an extraordinary private speech to the hierarchy of the South African police. In it, he said that for too long the police had been asked to solve South Africa's political problems. Henceforth this must be a task for the political leaders. For the ensuing unrest had been like a bush fire: if stamped out in one part of the veld, it simply flared up in another. More fighting would not lead to victory, but to racial conflagration. 'For if this Armageddon takes place – and blood flows ankle-deep in our streets and four or five million people lie dead – the problem will remain exactly the same as it was before the shooting started.'

On 23 January, I had an hour's talk with De Klerk on his own. In fact, all our conversations were just the two of us, as later my meetings were with Mandela. De Klerk said that he was addressing all the obstacles to getting negotiations under way – Mandela, the state of emergency and the ANC's commitment to the armed struggle (abandonment of which most of his colleagues wanted to be the quid pro quo for unbanning them).

I said that I did not see how any progress could be made without announcing an intention to release Mandela and unbanning the ANC. There would then be huge pressure on them to give up the armed struggle. I believed that De Klerk had reached this conclusion himself. I also said that it would make a hugely positive impact to announce suspension of the death penalty, which I knew he was also contemplating.

De Klerk stressed the importance of a helpful western response. He had raised this with the Americans, without getting any positive reply. I said that if he took these steps, there would be a positive response from us.

At midnight on 1 February 1990, De Klerk telephoned me at the embassy in Cape Town to say, 'You can tell your Prime Minister that she will not be disappointed.' I thanked him for forewarning us and told 10 Downing Street that the ANC and all other banned organisations would be unbanned, Mandela's release would follow shortly, the death penalty would be reviewed and there would be a justiciable declaration of rights in the new constitution.

*   *   *

On 2 February 1990, we gathered in our morning suits, the ladies all in hats, for the opening of Parliament, to listen to the speech that, as De Klerk observed beforehand, would change South Africa for ever. Andries Treurnicht and his Conservative Party cohorts walked out as De Klerk announced the unbanning of the ANC and the South African Communist Party, the freeing of political prisoners and the suspension of capital punishment. Then came the announcement the world had been waiting for. 'I wish to put it plainly that the government has taken a firm decision to release Mr Mandela unconditionally.'

While there had been much speculation, precious few had believed that De Klerk would be prepared to go this far. One of my friends in the ANC, Cheryl Carolus, was making a fiery speech to a huge crowd in Greenmarket Square at the time, urging them to march on Parliament, an idea that had to be abandoned when she heard, to her amazement, what De Klerk had done.

The Prime Minister congratulated De Klerk on this fundamental change of direction, opening the way for negotiations on a new constitution. She said that we would be reviewing the ban on new investment in South Africa. He replied, 'I can assure you that Nelson Mandela shortly will be a free man.'

A few days later, 10 Downing Street and I were given a few hours' notice of his release. The Prime Minister declared that instead of discouraging contacts with South Africa, henceforth we would be encouraging them. We were alone in doing so.

CHAPTER XIX

THE REAL MANDELA

The portrait of Nelson Mandela to be found in these pages is not the conventional hagiography. He could be dogmatic and distressingly partisan. Egged on by his colleagues in the ANC, he was at times unfair to De Klerk and forgetful of what he owed him. As he confessed to me, he made a major mistake in failing for nearly a year after his release to meet Chief Mangosuthu Buthelezi, the Zulu leader of Inkatha, who had refused to negotiate with the government so long as Mandela remained in jail.

Yet my admiration for him was second to no one's. As Desmond Tutu observed of him, this diamond had just one flaw, which was to put his trust in colleagues who did not always deserve it. He did so not just out of loyalty, but from political calculation. Mandela was conscious of the fears of his ANC colleagues in Lusaka that he might start negotiating with the government on his own and also that the township youth and half his colleagues had far more radical agendas than he did. This led him at times to engage in rhetoric and defend positions he did not really believe in, pandering deliberately to keep them on his side and under some measure of control.

Mandela was a far wilier politician, and could be less saintly, than some other portraits would have us believe, though he did indeed have some saintly characteristics. For at the time there were two Mandelas: in public, much of the time, there was the harshly aggressive, apparently unquestioning, spokesman of his party, reading out speeches written for him by the apparatchiks; and then there was the authentic Mandela, generous in spirit, libertarian by instinct, and inspirational to everyone he met. He used this dual personality quite deliberately to keep his supporters in line behind him. When the chips were down, as in his response to the assassination of Chris Hani, it was the real Mandela who took the stage.

The reader will find in this series of exchanges with him a fundamental difference of approach between Mandela and those of his colleagues whose overriding objective was to win power and hold on to it. Much as he revered the ANC, Mandela, as he showed in government, did not believe in the supremacy of the party over the judiciary and the press. He told Helen Suzman that he did not want his party to win a two-thirds majority in the first democratic elections, as he wanted there to be no temptation

LEFT Robin Renwick speech in Johannesburg, February 1988. 'If you want to get out of a hole, the first thing to do is to stop digging.' © *BUSINESS DAY*

BELOW Mandela with Helen Suzman in March 1990, shortly after his release from prison. © PICTURENET

Mandela's first meal in a restaurant for twenty-seven years, April 1990. © SUE CHARLTON

With Mandela at the British Embassy in Washington, March 1994.

ABOVE South African Foreign Minister Pik Botha peering through a telescope rescued from the wreck of HMS *Birkenhead*.
© GALLO IMAGES

LEFT US Navy pilot George Bush being rescued from the Pacific by a passing US submarine, 2 September 1944.
© GEORGE BUSH PRESIDENTIAL LIBRARY AND MUSEUM

With President Clinton at the British Embassy in Washington, June 1993.

to change the constitution. The least power-hungry of political leaders, he flatly refused to serve more than one term as President.

At the end of every meeting I had with him, he would never fail to ask for money for the ANC, as he was programmed by his colleagues to do, requests which I repeatedly declined. Central to the political magic of Mandela was his attitude to his actual or potential adversaries. Far from wishing or seeking to pick fights with them, his entire strategy was based on seeking to co-opt them. In prison he learned Afrikaans the better to understand the psychology of his adversaries. His warder ended up acting as his personal servant. The Justice Minister, Kobie Coetsee, kept asking me to help get him released. On his release from prison, I found him co-opting me.

When General Constand Viljoen was threatening a coup, he was invited to tea with Mandela, with Mandela of course serving the tea. He was persuaded instead to participate in the elections, in which his party fared very poorly.

Desmond Tutu became very disillusioned with the ANC. Mandela never allowed himself to be. He kept insisting to me that he was the servant of his party, not its master. It was, he contended, not a political party, but a movement to which all South Africans could belong. He kept urging me to join it myself – a curious offer to make to Thatcher's envoy. It was, he contended, a broad church 'and you think like us'. I told him that I thought like him, but not like a lot of his colleagues. He defended some of its worst transgressions, assuming personal responsibility for the indefensible shooting of Zulu Inkatha supporters demonstrating outside the ANC headquarters in Shell House, in which in reality he had no involvement at all.

So how was he able to disarm so many of his actual or potential opponents and bring his colleagues, however grudgingly, to accept a constitution to which many of them are no more than half reconciled today? The subsequent struggle by those opposed to Jacob Zuma was fought out in the name of a return to Mandela values, which was the most powerful slogan there could have been.

For this was a leader who was not just admired but loved by his people of all races and by those of us who were co-opted by him. We could see through his multiple subterfuges, but they were almost always in a good cause. He thought very little about himself, but was determined to leave his country in a much better place and to seek to redress the evils of the past without compromising the future. His last words to me, when the land invasions were being orchestrated in Zimbabwe, were, 'If the same thing started here, I would come out of retirement and stop it on the first farm.'

The account that follows of my exchanges with him is

not based on memory, but on the reports I sent to the Foreign Office at the time, to which they kindly allowed me access to help ensure its accuracy.

CHAPTER XX

'HE IS A BIGGER MAN THAN THE OTHERS AND THIS WILL SHOW'

On arriving in South Africa in 1987, I had struggled with the problem of making any kind of contact with Nelson Mandela. But his great friend, and mine, Helen Suzman was occasionally permitted to see him. She knew the efforts we were making to secure his release, but I wanted her to hear this direct from the Prime Minister, which she did in two meetings with her in Downing Street. Helen saw Mandela when he was hospitalised for a lung infection and, thereafter, on two occasions when he was moved to prison in Paarl.

When she had lunch with him there, she found Mandela installed in a warder's cottage in the prison grounds, with the lunch being cooked and served by the warder, Warrant Officer Swart, who also was trying in vain to stop Mandela from making his own bed. But he was still a prisoner and she told him about the efforts we were making to try to help secure his release.

I reported to London that, through his lawyer, Hymie Bernhardt, Mandela had thanked me for the help we were giving to people in the townships. This found its way into the British press as a supposed message from him to Mrs Thatcher.

In response, I received a manuscript letter on prison notepaper from Nelson Mandela. This said that if he had wished to comment on Mrs Thatcher's work or the policy of the British government, 'I would have preferred to do so in the course of a face-to-face discussion with you. Meanwhile, I am happy to request you to pass my very best wishes to the Prime Minister.'

As De Klerk by now was taking over from P. W. Botha, I was permitted to reply. I said that the Prime Minister's position was well known. It was that he should be freed and free to express his views. I looked forward to a face-to-face discussion with him and so did she. We were continuing our efforts to promote a negotiation in which all parties could take part.

*　*　*

On the day of his release, Mandela met with a tumultuous and chaotic reception in Cape Town, his car barely able to get through to City Hall. On this great day, I was delighted to have staying with me Anthony and Sally Sampson. Anthony, a friend of Mandela since before he was sent to jail and of Oliver Tambo, had done much to help with my own contacts with the ANC, at a time when we were imagined not to be talking to them. This never was the case, as my colleagues in Lusaka had long-standing relationships with Thabo Mbeki and his colleagues there, including Jacob Zuma, and Anthony arranged a couple of private meetings for me with Tambo.

Mandela's speech on the day of his release fell a long way short of matching the historic occasion. Described by the *Financial Times* correspondent Patti Waldmeir as 'a speech from hell', amidst a welter of hardline rhetoric, it stressed the need to continue the armed struggle, intensify sanctions and pursue nationalisation, though he did declare that De Klerk was a man of integrity.

While these were all ANC mantras, the entire emphasis was backward and not forward looking. It took me some time to discover what had happened. The speech turned out to have been amended by Winnie Mandela, causing a delay before he walked out of the Victor Verster Prison.

On the following day, the real voice of Mandela was heard during a press conference in the gardens of Archbishop Tutu's house in Bishopscourt. He said that the ANC were concerned to address white fears over one person, one vote: 'The whites are our fellow South Africans. We want them to feel safe.' He recognised their contribution to the development of the country.

*   *   *

Four days later, I was greeted with great friendliness by Mandela at a first meeting in Johannesburg. To the surprise of the attendant television crews, he asked for his best wishes to be passed to the Prime Minister.

In a meeting with the western Ambassadors, he said that for years he had been seeking to achieve a negotiation between the government and the ANC. South Africa was fortunate to have De Klerk as its head of state. But apartheid still existed and sanctions should be maintained.

He concluded by asking for help specifically from us. Mrs Thatcher had led the way in persuading Gorbachev and Reagan that they could do business together. These were breathtaking developments.

I said that we were urging the government to remove all the remaining obstacles to negotiations. There would shortly be an amnesty. We believed that they would soon lift the state of emergency. We were urging them to think not of group but of minority rights, the term Mandela himself was using. We hoped that, once negotiations started, the armed struggle would be suspended.

As Mandela referred to the case of the Boer leader General Christiaan de Wet in arguing for the release of prisoners, I told him that I had several times used the same example with P. W. Botha in arguing for his own release.

Mandela asked for help with Pik Botha in getting a passport for him to meet his ANC colleagues in Lusaka. Pik Botha assured me that this would be delivered immediately.

At a meeting in Soweto with Walter Sisulu, who had been appointed chairman of the internal wing of the ANC, and his deputy, Ahmed Kathrada, I said that we had urged De Klerk to take all these steps and had told him that if he did so there would be a response, at any rate from us. If he did not get one, it would be harder for him to go further. The arms, nuclear and oil embargoes would remain in place until apartheid was gone. We were not going to treat De Klerk as if he were P. W. Botha. Their own release, and that of Mandela, had owed a lot to pressure from the Prime Minister.

Both said that they were well aware of this and Kathrada had said so publicly. They hoped that we would not lead a crusade against sanctions. I said that we wouldn't, but at some point I would ask them to reconsider the sports boycott, as the best way of helping De Klerk.

Meanwhile I asked them to start reconsidering the

ANC policy on nationalisation, which hadn't worked anywhere. If the banks and mines were nationalised without
compensation, there would be no further investment in
the country.

These two highly impressive ANC leaders agreed to
reflect on this. It would, they said, have to be discussed
exhaustively within the ANC.

The next day, Walter Sisulu rang to say that Mandela
wanted to see me in Soweto. I met him in the tiny match-
box-size house he had returned to, not wanting at first
to move into his wife's much larger house in Diepkloof,
known to the Sowetans as 'Beverly Hills'.

The contrast was dramatic between these humble sur-
roundings and the quality of the man inside. Mandela in
this period had not yet adopted the batik shirts he later
made so famous, instead appearing in immaculate Prince
of Wales tweed suits made for him by his friend and tailor,
Yusuf Surtee.

His old-world courtesy and unfailing charm served to
mask a steely determination not to compromise any of
the principles for which he and his colleagues had sacrificed their liberty or lives. He was, he kept emphasising,
the servant of his party, not its master. He had difficulty
accepting that the ANC could be wrong, and even in understanding that others might not wish to join it.

Yet from the outset he showed a much greater

commitment to genuine political tolerance than many others in the ANC and acceptance that South Africa must be a society with which all sections of the population could identify, including his former oppressors.

Mandela said that he knew the role the Prime Minister had played and the efforts I had made to help secure his release and that of Walter Sisulu and the unbanning of the ANC. But international pressure must be maintained. I said that we agreed with this, but did so in a manner different to other countries, through direct engagement with the South African government. We were pressing them to lift the state of emergency and release all political prisoners.

But we could not agree with ANC demands for an interim government and that elections should be held to a constituent assembly before any agreement had been reached on the future constitution. They had no chance of being accepted and amounted to a demand that majority rule should be established before negotiations had taken place.

Mandela said he considered that only two conditions – lifting the state of emergency and an amnesty for political prisoners – needed to be met for negotiations to be engaged. I asked if, on that basis, the ANC would call off the armed struggle. Mandela felt that they should.

Mandela said that he had a high regard for the Prime

Minister and wanted to get her support. He would be attending the Wembley concert celebrating his release in London on 16 April. He had wanted to meet her then, but had to get the agreement of the ANC.

As the US oil giant Mobil recently had disinvested, leaving us being asked to bail out projects they had been supporting in Soweto, I asked Mandela not to call for further disinvestment, explaining why. Mandela said that he could not change the ANC line on disinvestment. I said that I was not asking him to; only that he should not call for it himself (and, as a matter of fact, he never did).

Mandela told me subsequently that he was annoyed with his colleagues for opposing a meeting with Mrs Thatcher during the Wembley visit and had told them that he would be meeting her on the next occasion.

Meanwhile, he needed some practical help from us. He asked us to provide training for his personal bodyguards, which we arranged for the SAS to do. Later on, when he moved into his wife's much larger house, he asked for our help in providing better privacy and security there.

*   *   *

As the violence continued in Natal, I urged Mandela to meet Mangosuthu Buthelezi, reminding him that Buthelezi had refused to negotiate with the government until Mandela was released. Mandela told me that he had telephoned Buthelezi and wanted to meet him. But this was opposed by the ANC leadership in Lusaka.

Mandela, addressing a huge crowd in Durban, urged them to 'take your guns, your knives and your pangas and throw them into the sea ... End this war now!'

But because of the opposition of the ANC war party in Natal, led by Harry Gwala, a planned meeting with Buthelezi was cancelled. Mandela told me that when he mentioned meeting Buthelezi at an ANC rally in Pietermaritzburg, he found the crowd openly opposing him.

The leading Zulu among the exiles, Jacob Zuma, agreed that Mandela's failure to meet Buthelezi for nearly a year after his release was a major mistake. It was only after the meeting eventually did take place that more serious efforts were made to end the violence, with Zuma at the time playing a constructive role in helping to do so.

Mandela was persuaded by his colleagues consistently to underestimate the Inkatha Freedom Party, led by Chief Buthelezi, quoting to me an *Economist* report that they only had 1 per cent support in the Witwatersrand townships. I said that when he did get around to meeting Buthelezi in Ulundi, he would find that in large areas of rural Zululand he had 100 per cent support. It came as a surprise to Mandela when Inkatha won in Natal in the 1994 elections.

When Buthelezi saw Mrs Thatcher in London, she expressed disappointment at the ANC's refusal to suspend the armed struggle and its commitment to nationalisation. Buthelezi said that Mandela was a bigger man than the others and eventually this would show.

And so it did, as Mandela later was to make amends, with Buthelezi as a Deputy President in his government and, on more than one occasion, designated as acting President when Mandela and Mbeki were overseas. Mandela subsequently declared, 'For more than ten years, we did everything we could to destroy Buthelezi – and we failed. He is a born political survivor!'

CHAPTER XXI

'FOR A POLITICAL LEADER WHO LOSES THE SUPPORT OF HIS FOLLOWERS, IT REMAINS ONLY TO WRITE HIS MEMOIRS'

Following police shootings in Sebokeng in March 1990, in which eleven people were killed, Mandela threatened to postpone indefinitely talks with the government. The police action was indefensible and was denounced by De Klerk, but over 400 people had been killed since the unbanning of the ANC and much of the mayhem had been caused by the teenage 'comrades'.

I had been asked by Mandela to lobby the government to release the ANC youth leader, Peter Mokaba. I did so, only for Mokaba to celebrate his release by making a 'One Boer, one bullet' speech in Nelspruit. When I remonstrated with Mandela he claimed, tongue in cheek, that 'the young man must have been misinterpreted'. I said that Mokaba needed to be told to shut up, failing which he would be re-arrested. The jackal-like Mokaba, much later, was to lead an attack on Mandela in the last ANC leadership meeting Mandela attended.

In March 1990, Douglas Hurd, the Foreign Secretary, and I found De Klerk reacting calmly to the difficulties around him. The sticking point for him was that the new constitution must provide protection for minority rights. In response to hardline statements by Mandela on behalf of the ANC, Hurd observed that, overseas, his pronouncements were greeted with near-universal reverence, whether or not they actually made sense.

De Klerk said that, for South Africa to sign the Nuclear Non-Proliferation Treaty, they needed our help in persuading their neighbours to do so as well, even though the effect, obviously, would be purely symbolic.

On a visit we arranged to some of the projects we were supporting in the Cape townships, Hurd was surprised to find himself being escorted around Crossroads by an honour guard of young black South Africans carrying wooden rifles and chanting 'Viva Tambo!', but he took this in his stride.

As we moved on to the Namibian independence celebrations, Hurd concluded that De Klerk, bent on dismantling apartheid and the South African nuclear programme, was 'an amazingly brave and wise man'.

In Windhoek, the Soviet Foreign Minister, Eduard Shevardnadze, commented favourably on his meeting with De Klerk. We should use our relationship with the South African government, and the Russians would use theirs with the ANC.

On return to South Africa, I asked Roelf Meyer, who was increasingly involved in the government's dealings with the ANC, whether the state of emergency could not be restricted to Natal. Could they not also set about re-pealing all the remaining apartheid laws?

Mandela arrived in London for the Wembley concert celebrating his release. Seventy-two thousand people attended the star-studded concert, which was broad-cast to more than sixty countries. Mandela received an eight-minute standing ovation when he took the stage.

Margaret Thatcher reacted with understandable in-credulity to a statement by him (on behalf of the ANC) criticising her planned further meeting with F. W. De Klerk, whom she had helped to persuade to release him. But Mandela also said publicly that he would be returning to London to meet her and, as he had told me, that she was 'a very powerful lady – one I would much rather have on my side'.

Pik Botha told me that the Population Registration Act, cornerstone of the apartheid system, classifying all South Africans by race, would fall away automatically with a new constitution. I said that it would be far better to repeal it beforehand.

Neil van Heerden said there was evidence that not everyone in the ANC was committed to a negotiated solution. I said that they were making exactly the same point about the security forces.

The overthrow of the intensely unpopular homeland government in Ciskei, in the south-east of South Africa, was followed by scenes of looting and arson. I asked Terror Lekota of the ANC to help put a stop to this, given that we wanted to see an end to the state of emergency, which Lekota did help to do.

At the first meeting between the government and the ANC, held at the historic 'Groote Schuur' ('great barn') residence of Cecil Rhodes in Cape Town, the two sides got on better than many had expected.

Mandela told an astonished crowd in Soweto that they needed to learn Afrikaans. I recalled, to laughter from Mandela, that the last political leader to suggest this had been Dr Andries Treurnicht, whose attempt to introduce Afrikaans in schools had triggered the 1976 Soweto riots.

Mandela continued to stick to ANC demands for a constituent assembly, which had no chance of being accepted. It was clear that he knew this himself. But, in a revealing aside, he told me that he was where he was because of the organisation, adding, 'For a political leader who lost the support of his followers, it would remain only to write his memoirs.' It was precisely for this reason that he never hesitated to read out hardline statements written for him by the ANC and toured the world unashamedly demanding, from everyone he met, funds for the party, while invariably seeking compromise himself.

I suggested that, to celebrate his release, we should meet for lunch in the best restaurant in Johannesburg, at the time Linger Longer in Braamfontein. There was a sharp intake of breath on the part of the proprietor as we revealed, at the last minute, the identity of my guest, followed by astonishment on the part of the other diners, most of whom had voted to keep him in jail, as Mandela went from table to table greeting them as if they were his natural supporters. It was a bravura performance, often to be repeated, calculated to win over his former opponents. At the end of the meal, characteristically, he dived into the kitchen to thank those who had prepared it.

De Klerk announced the lifting of the state of emergency everywhere except in Natal and agreement was reached on the release of prisoners. But the ANC still were clinging to the notion of the armed struggle and to nationalisation.

CHAPTER XXII

'HOW DO I GET HER ON MY SIDE?'

In each of his meetings with me, I had found Mandela practising his classic strategy of seeking to co-opt me, just as he had his warder in jail and the Justice Minister. The journalist John Carlin, who has written more perceptively than anyone about Mandela, in *Playing the Enemy* and *Knowing Mandela*, describes the same tactics being used on him. I was his adviser, Mandela kept insisting to me and others. I soon found that his next target for co-option was more ambitious. It was in fact the Prime Minister.

Mandela was planning to visit the United States, to be followed by a visit to London to see Mrs Thatcher. He called to ask me to meet him at a private clinic in Johannesburg. He had been admitted suffering from exhaustion.

I told him that we were extremely worried about his schedule in the US, where he was due to visit seven cities in ten days. To give him some rest en route, we were arranging for him to spend a quiet weekend in the English countryside with his friend Oliver Tambo.

What he wanted to talk about was how to tackle Margaret Thatcher. He wanted her as an ally and not as an enemy.

I suggested that we should have a rehearsal for the meeting. 'You can be Mandela,' I said, 'and I'll be Mrs Thatcher.'

There followed an exchange punctuated by much laughter on both sides. Mandela described the efforts he and Tambo had made to engage with the government before he was convicted of treason and that all they now wanted was a fully democratic constitution. 'You will find us firm allies on that,' I said, 'but you must stop all this nonsense about nationalising the banks and the mines.'

'But it was your idea!' he said, referring to the influence of the London School of Economics on budding African politicians in the 1960s. 'It was fashionable then,' he added with a smile. It was not fashionable now, I replied, even in the Soviet Union.

I added that, personally, I did not believe that the ANC would end up nationalising anything. We had just been through all this with SWAPO. Nationalisation had failed everywhere it had been tried in Africa. Mandela thanked me for these 'tips' for his meeting with Margaret Thatcher.

During his stay with Tambo, Mandela telephoned her. He said that she had played a great part in helping to secure his release and that of his colleagues and persuading the government to sit down and negotiate with them. She urged him to give up the armed struggle. He said that the government did not seem able to control sections of the police. But he was committed to a negotiated outcome.

I reported to No. 10 that, in his meeting with her, Mandela wanted to establish a personal rapport, 'which should not be difficult, given the character of the man'.

* * *

I saw Margaret Thatcher in 10 Downing Street before Mandela arrived. 'Please remember', I said, 'that he has waited twenty-seven years to tell you his story.' This earned me a stare from the clear blue eyes. 'You mean I mustn't interrupt?' she said. Not for the first half-hour, I suggested. Asked if Mandela was anything like Robert Mugabe, I was able to assure her that I had never met two human beings, let alone political leaders, less like each other than Nelson Mandela and Robert Mugabe.

Mandela arrived in the rain, with a mild case of pneumonia. The Prime Minister attempted to revive him with a small glass of port. 'She chided me like a schoolmarm for not cutting down on my schedule,' he observed. She then listened for more than an hour as Mandela explained the history of the ANC and the difficulties he was facing in negotiations. She found him, as she wrote in her memoirs, 'supremely courteous, with a genuine nobility of bearing and – most remarkable after all that he had suffered – without any bitterness'.

She promised support in achieving a fully democratic constitution. She urged him to suspend the armed struggle and to meet Buthelezi. Also to stop talking about nationalising the banks and the mines (provoking a grin from him to me), which would frighten away all new investment.

Mandela by this stage had abandoned the idea of a constituent assembly and said that the ANC had not decided on nationalisation. They wanted to work with the business community.

As, to her, he still seemed stuck in 'some kind of socialist time warp', she launched into a discussion of basic economics, with his deputy, Thabo Mbeki, clearly agreeing with her.

Charles Powell, in his report on the meeting, noted that Mandela's initial remarks had lasted, uninterrupted, for over fifty minutes, 'possibly a record'. The meeting had gone on for three hours, causing the press assembled outside in Downing Street to start chanting 'Free Nelson Mandela!'

Mandela went on to see the Labour Party leader, Neil Kinnock, who asked how he had got on with Thatcher. 'She was warm and motherly,' said Mandela. 'You must have met some other lady,' Kinnock protested.

At his press conference that afternoon, choosing his words with heavy emphasis, Mandela declared, 'She *is* an enemy of apartheid.' He had come away from the meeting full of hope. His reaction, as he said slyly to me afterwards, was that she was 'a woman he could do business with'.

A few months later, when Margaret Thatcher was defenestrated by her colleagues in the Conservative Party, Mandela told the BBC that while they had disagreed about strategy, in particular sanctions, 'we have much to be thankful to her for'.

CHAPTER XXIII

'THE ONLY ALTERNATIVE TO NEGOTIATIONS NOW IS NEGOTIATIONS LATER'

With the ANC still in a state of extreme disorganisation, there followed an episode much appreciated by my colleagues. Having arranged to meet Mandela one afternoon at his party headquarters in Johannesburg, I found that he had gone to meet me at the British embassy in Pretoria – where the embassy staff were thrilled to have the opportunity to meet the great man.

As I kept urging the ANC leaders to suspend the armed struggle, I found an unexpected ally in the South African Communist Party leader, Joe Slovo. Despite the misgivings of his wife, Ruth First (assassinated by a bomb despatched by the security police in 1982), he had defended every twist and turn of Soviet policy since the Second World War. Yet face to face I found him quite a genial, would-be avuncular, character, with a clearer grasp of strategy than many of his colleagues. He understood the need, he said, to demonstrate to De Klerk and others that they were negotiating in good faith.

Having concerted this with Mandela, it was Slovo who persuaded his colleagues to announce the suspension of the armed struggle. This was agreed despite some continuing opposition, for, as Mandela observed, the armed struggle had gained among ANC supporters a popularity far beyond what had been achieved on the ground.

Mandela by now was telling me that he was exhausted and planned to go to Cuba for three weeks' holiday and medical treatment. I said that he had just made a very successful visit to the United States. To follow this immediately with three weeks with Fidel Castro would be a mistake. Why not take a holiday in South Africa, with his and my friend Enos Mabuza in KaNgwane, on the edge of the Kruger Park, alongside the game reserve of Londolozi?

This was a great success. He resisted appeals from Winnie ('Come back, we are at war') to return to Soweto. I arrived at the embassy one morning to be told that Mandela was trying to reach me. Imagining some new crisis in negotiations, I rang him back, only to be given the politically incorrect news that he had succeeded in shooting an antelope.

Mandela confirmed that he would drop the idea of a constituent assembly. I was urging the ANC and the government to start working on the future constitutional principles. The process risked being derailed by the violence in the townships. Mandela said that he was telling ANC supporters not to attack Inkatha-supporting Zulu hostel dwellers. But elements of the police were supporting or conniving at violence against the ANC. He still wanted to meet Buthelezi, but could not do so at the risk of a split in his party.

I said that I was glad that De Klerk had been given a good reception when he visited Soweto. Mandela agreed. I believed that De Klerk was close to announcing his intention to repeal all the remaining apartheid legislation and to open the National Party to people of all races, thereby transforming its nature completely. He needed to be helped to retain the support of his constituency. The ANC did not want to lift other sanctions, but I would be asking them to consider lifting sports sanctions in cases where the governing bodies of the sports now were integrated.

I was conscious that, among his overseas contacts, I was the one who spent some of the time arguing with him. The others came mainly to worship at the shrine. Nearly all our meetings were attended by just him and me. When he returned from a visit to Libya, however, I went to see him with our mutual friend Helen Suzman. I suggested as politely as I could that it was not a good idea to have called Colonel Gaddafi a great supporter of human rights, only to be interrupted by Helen Suzman. 'How could you be so silly, Nelson?' she enquired. A Mandela statement that the vote should be extended to fourteen-year-olds earned him another 'Don't be silly, Nelson' call from her. As she lambasted the ANC for its misdeeds as heartily as she had their predecessors, he said that he was beginning to feel sorry for her opponents in the National Party.

As the ANC still contended that Inkatha were responsible for all the violence, I handed Mandela a photograph of a group of young 'comrades' necklacing a Zulu hostel dweller. Mandela said, 'These are not our people.' I pointed to the ANC logos on their T-shirts.

In his statements overseas, Mandela continued to attribute the violence entirely to the security forces. I said that, as a friend, I hoped that he would not do so now that he had returned. I and other members of the embassy were regular visitors to the townships, as were members of the British press. There were many incidents of violence in which ANC youth were attacking the representatives of other political parties. It would be damaging to his own reputation to go on pretending that they were blameless.

Following these exchanges, Mandela did start making occasional statements referring to violence from all sides, but it was not until 1993 that he fully acknowledged that 'there are members of the ANC who are killing our own people. We must face the truth. Our people are just as involved as other organisations in committing violence.'

In another sign of a return to normality, the Foreign Affairs Committee of the House of Commons descended on us in South Africa. I invited them to a dinner in Pretoria at which the entire political spectrum of South Africa was represented, causing the editor of *City Press* to ask why this could only happen in a foreign embassy: they needed to start doing this themselves.

They wanted to see Mandela, who insisted that I must get there first and sit on his side of the table, so that I could be introduced as his adviser! They applauded the township projects, suggesting that this model should be adopted elsewhere in Africa. (Far from this suggestion being adopted, the projects we had been supporting were wound up, once our aid department took over, in favour of cheques to the government.)

In November 1990, Mr Justice Harms, who was supposed to investigate the horrendous misdeeds of the so-called Civil Cooperation Bureau and the assassination squad at Vlakplaas, produced a pathetic report, causing De Klerk to start relying on a much tougher judge, Richard Goldstone.

In December, Oliver and Adelaide Tambo returned to South Africa. I received a message from the very

Anglophile Tambos, summoning me to meet them in Soweto, as they wanted, they said, to meet 'our Ambassador'. I was very pleased to be described in those terms by them. For, in my meetings with him in London, I had found Oliver Tambo to be far more of a statesman than most of his colleagues. It was a tragedy for South Africa that he was by then so frail, as he would have made a huge contribution, if he had had the chance to do so, in the post-apartheid government.

His ideas were the same as those of his lifelong friend Mandela. While Adelaide already had found a local source of currant cake, he told me that he planned to urge Mandela to meet Buthelezi and that at the ANC preparatory conference, he intended to call for the ANC's sanctions policy to be reconsidered. It was no use demanding that De Klerk should be treated as if he were P. W. Botha. This went down badly with the overheated delegates. Mandela too was criticised for 'personal diplomacy'.

A meeting with Buthelezi at last was agreed in January 1991. I told Mandela that I had seen his statement in Lusaka that if negotiations failed, the ANC would have to 'seize power'.

I told him that we did not believe that they were in a position to seize power (and nor did he). If negotiations broke down, they would simply have to be started up again. Mandela said that he agreed. He was pleased at the remarkable improvement in relations between Britain and the ANC and the role the embassy had played in this. He regarded us as 'the principal supporters of the negotiating process'.

In February, De Klerk announced the repeal of all the remaining apartheid laws. At a dinner with him afterwards, he was confident he could win a referendum of the white electorate. What would help him most with them would be a rugby tour! The ANC were backing away from nationalisation. Mandela could be rigid and dogmatic, but he had to straddle two very different tendencies – radical and more moderate – within the ANC.

*　　*　　*

In April, Mandela accused the government of complicity in the violence in the black communities and demanded a ban on the carrying of traditional weapons and the phasing out of the all-male mineworkers' hostels, many of which were Zulu Inkatha strongholds. If these demands were not met by 9 May, the ANC would break off negotiations and discussion of a new constitution.

Mandela's accusations about security force collusion in some of the attacks on the ANC undoubtedly were true. De Klerk was unable to control elements of the security forces, with the connivance of their superiors, who hated what he was doing. What Mandela failed to admit was that many of these clashes were provoked by ANC youth and so-called self-defence units.

To try to help break the deadlock at this time, I had another lunch with Joe Slovo. The government had offered a commission of inquiry. It would take many years to phase out the all-male hostels. There would be no sympathy for anyone who broke off negotiations. The need rather was to accelerate them. 'The only alternative to negotiations now', I said to him, as I had to Mandela, 'is negotiations later.'

Slovo largely agreed. It was a mistake for the ANC to have declared their demands to be an 'ultimatum'. He acknowledged that the violence was not benefiting De Klerk.

On 6 May, I telephoned Mandela at his house in Soweto. I told him that we knew that De Klerk had never ordered the killing of anyone, any more than Mandela had done. We had pressed the government to order an inquiry, headed by a judge. The ANC should accept this.

Mandela said that he was talking to De Klerk, as was Mbeki. A few days later, at a jazz evening at the home of our mutual friend Clive Menell, Mandela said that De Klerk must do more to curb the security forces, but negotiations would be resumed.

A few weeks earlier, some shots had been fired at the

embassy office in Pretoria, albeit on a Sunday and without doing any harm. This was the work of a *bittereinder* Afrikaner faction led by Piet 'Skiet' Rudolph. By now I was being denounced in the right-wing Afrikaans propaganda sheets as, improbably, the reincarnation of Lord Milner, bent on the destruction of the Boers.

CHAPTER XXIV

'WE CAN HARDLY DROP THEM ON LUSAKA OR SOWETO'

The other cause we had been trying to pursue through-out my time in South Africa was to persuade the government to sign the Nuclear Non-Proliferation Treaty and to destroy its small arsenal of nuclear bombs. This was no small ask as, hitherto, no other country had been pre-pared to do this. The Americans too were working actively in this cause.

I found a powerful ally in the Finance Minister, Barend du Plessis. The military nuclear programme by now had cost nearly a billion dollars. He could not understand what use South Africa could possibly make of nuclear weapons. 'We can', as he said to me, 'hardly drop them on Lusaka or Soweto.' Since the inception of the programme in 1974, South Africa had managed to produce six and a half Hiroshima-type atomic bombs. Their scientists were confident that these would work, though no tests had been conducted.

De Klerk had come to the same conclusion. The programme had been supposed to deter the 'total onslaught' by the Soviet Union and its surrogates. One of De Klerk's first acts after becoming President was to order the decommissioning of the enrichment plant near Pretoria at Pelindaba – a Zulu word variously translated as 'end of the discussion' or 'where important matters are settled'.

*   *   *

Mandela, meanwhile, was greatly affected by the trial of his wife, accused of the kidnapping and assault in December 1988 of Stompie Moeketsi and three other young men. The fourteen-year-old Moeketsi was murdered by Winnie Mandela's bodyguard, a member of the so-called Mandela United Football Club, which had been conducting a reign of terror in Soweto.

Mandela kept telling me, and even maintained in his autobiography, *Long Walk to Freedom*, that she was innocent. As I remained silent, he would add that, anyway, he was responsible, having left her on her own for twenty-seven years. It was her infidelity, and not her other misdeeds, that caused Mandela to break with Winnie.

As my time as Ambassador was drawing to a close, I

went to Bloemfontein to see the humane and wise Chief Justice Corbett, head of the Supreme Court. I said that, while Winnie Mandela might well be found guilty, I doubted if Mandela would be able to cope if his wife were sent to prison. The Justice Minister, Kobie Coetsee, said the same to other members of the judiciary. In the event, she received a suspended sentence.

As De Klerk was now planning a referendum of the white community on his policies, I asked to see Mandela, with, this time, his spokesman on sport, Steve Tshwete, also attending. I argued for a selective easing of the sports boycott. Mandela, an ardent sports fan and a believer in sport as a unifying factor, responded positively. He and his colleagues, he said, were thinking on similar lines. A few weeks later, the ANC agreed to the re-admission of South Africa to international cricket and Olympic sport. De Klerk felt that the fact that a South African cricket team was touring Australia did help him in his referendum.

*   *   *

Margaret Thatcher by this time had been replaced as Prime Minister by John Major. Through four years in South Africa, I had received no instructions but plenty of support from her. The Foreign Office didn't send me any instructions either, as they were wary that she might not agree with them. I was helped by the fact that the senior official responsible for Africa, Patrick Fairweather, was a close friend.

Her faults were of the same dimension as her virtues. She had governed not as a chairman, but as an increasingly imperious CEO, making life at times impossible for her ministers, as she did later for her successor. But Noel Annan, himself a luminary of the liberal intellectual establishment, expressed to me, as he did also in his book *Our Age*, his dismay at the intensity of their antagonism to this 'remarkable woman, far less hollow than her predecessors', whose accomplishments far exceeded theirs.

She never seemed to me, in any way, a typical Tory leader, being far too much of a radical for that, interested in ideas, determined to move mountains, conscious that she 'offended on many counts', as being 'not just of a different sex, but of a different class'. None of my close acquaintances in the government at the time – Peter Carrington, Ian Gilmour and Christopher Soames – thought that she had any chance of defeating the trade unions, transforming the economy and exporting privatisation around the world.

In the previous two years, for all her stamina and ferocious energy, she had been suffering from cumulative fatigue. While the time had come for her to go, I also felt that there were ways – her fearlessness, clarity of purpose and utter absence of wishful thinking – in which one day she might be badly missed.

De Klerk regarded it as a debt of honour to invite her to visit South Africa. The ANC Youth League didn't like it, but she got an enthusiastic reception at the Baragwanath Hospital when, with Helen Suzman, I took her to visit Soweto. She concluded her tour by asking me a question to which I still do not have the answer. Given that the independence constitutions in much of the rest of Africa had been honoured more in the breach than in the observance, did I believe that governments in Africa were prepared to accept the western notion, dating from the eighteenth century, that it was in their own interests to limit their own power and that, however irksome a free press and independent judiciary might be, the alternative was worse?

South Africa recently passed this test, by electing as President Cyril Ramaphosa, who negotiated the constitution and is committed to it. But the ruling party did so by a wafer-thin majority. Ramaphosa's problems will come not from his opponents but from his colleagues within the ANC.

On leaving South Africa, I travelled to Pretoria to attend a farewell party given by my deputy, Anthony Rowell, who had forged his own close links with Mbeki and Zuma. I arrived to find Mandela there, together with his wife, who was in ebullient form, having managed to get herself arrested twice earlier in the day. I was described by the amused British press as 'struggling in her embrace'.

I told Mandela that we were concerned that the ANC should not paint themselves into a corner by making non-negotiable demands at their conference in Durban. So were Mbeki and Zuma, alarmed at the temporary ascendancy of the radical wing of the ANC, represented by Chris Hani, Winnie and the township youth. I asked where the demand that De Klerk should hand over power forthwith to an interim government had come from. Mandela asked me to send him a note about this, which on the next day I did. Mandela ensured that the demand was dropped by the ANC.

De Klerk removed General Malan from his post as Defence Minister and Adriaan Vlok from his post as Minister of Law and Order. A report by a much tougher judge than Justice Harms, Richard Goldstone, led to the dismissal of several generals. The head of the Defence Force was replaced by General Georg Meiring. When the former head of the army, General Constand Viljoen, said that they could take over the country in an afternoon, Meiring replied, 'Yes. And what would we do then?'

Goldstone's report declared that, notwithstanding the contribution made to it by elements of the security forces, the 'primary cause' of the violence was the political rivalry between the ANC and Inkatha. Mandela professed to find this conclusion 'superficial'.

* * *

Having talked to all the political leaders in my last few days in South Africa, I left convinced that the negotiation process was indeed irreversible and that agreement would be reached on a democratic constitution.

I had been extremely fortunate in my timing. My predecessors, however hard they tried – and some tried harder than others – could not hope to achieve much in the face of that ironclad regime. And what in the end was achieved was accomplished by and for South Africans, not by any outsider, however well disposed. The most that any embassy could do was to act as a facilitator. For a time, the South African government, trying hard to change, did feel that it needed one western country to confide in. For a time, Mandela and the ANC did feel that they needed someone with, they hoped, some influence on the other side. Within months, there would be no further need or scope for such a role.

*   *   *

I had discussed with Mandela the impossibility of improving living standards for the majority of South Africans until there was a return of investment into the country. I had promised that as soon as he was ready to call for new investment, I would do what I could to promote this.

As the first ever one person, one vote elections

approached, Mandela asked me to arrange a dinner at the British embassy in Washington to appeal to international investors to return.

I invited a galaxy of US businessmen and fund managers. Mandela arrived with the usual dreadful speech prepared for him by the ANC. I persuaded him to discard this and instead to announce that he would be meeting Buthelezi and intended to ask De Klerk's respected Finance Minister, Derek Keys, to continue in his post.

I pointed out to Mandela that several of the South African businessmen travelling in his wake had been pillars of the apartheid regime. Mandela replied that he forgave nothing, and nor did he forget, but he needed them now.

When Mandela made his state visit to Britain in 1996, he combined with the Prince of Wales to organise a musical evening at the Albert Hall. Asked to look after him at half-time, I pointed out that when it came to the performance by Ladysmith Black Mambazo, the entire audience would be expecting him to stand up and dance, as he did in South Africa. Mandela was worried that this might upset the Queen, whom he greatly admired and was in the habit of addressing as 'Elizabeth'. But get up and dance he did, with the Duke of Edinburgh following suit – and then the Queen.

Not long after, I was annoyed to hear from his friend Anthony Sampson that Mandela had started saying that he preferred dealing with P. W. Botha than De Klerk, whom the ANC still saw as a political rival. Meeting Mandela in his office in Cape Town, I recalled that in that same office I had argued with P. W. Botha several times for his release, with no success. I also had been obliged to argue for the lives of some of his supporters. But for De Klerk, he might still be in jail.

Mandela, laughing, said that I was right. De Klerk had deserved his Nobel Peace Prize, for he it was who had made peace possible.

*   *   *

When Mandela retired as President after just one term, he found his successor, Thabo Mbeki, desperate to step out from his shadow. Mandela told me that he could get through to any President in the world except his own, who did not return his phone calls.

They disagreed about Zimbabwe. Mandela detested Mugabe, whom he used to refer to derisively as 'Comrade Bob'. Asked what should be done about him, on one occasion Mandela said, 'If necessary, take up arms,' bringing him some violent remonstrances from the ANC.

But Mandela and Mbeki's far more serious disagreement was about Aids. This led Mandela to discover that his intense loyalty to his party was not always reciprocated.

Having criticised the failure to take action against the epidemic, he was summoned to a meeting of the ANC's National Executive Committee. Mbeki did not attend, but Mandela was attacked in insulting terms by a claque of Mbeki supporters. Mandela never attended another leadership meeting of the ANC.

He certainly was not happy at the endemic corruption and race-based propaganda under Jacob Zuma, with their last photo together showing a frail Mandela very ill at ease. But he still could not bring himself to criticise his party, to whom he felt a higher loyalty. It was left to Kgalema Motlanthe, interim President of South Africa between Mbeki and Zuma, to point out to his colleagues, 'We did not join the ANC to get rich. We joined it to go to jail.'

*　*　*

When, under Jacob Zuma, there were good reasons to be pessimistic about South Africa, John Carlin, author of *Invictus*, observed to me: 'Never forget, it is a magnificent country!'

And a magnificent country it is, with some magnificent people within it, among them the fearless Public Protector, Thuli Madonsela, who did more than anyone to bring Jacob Zuma to account. With her habitual careful choice of language, she thanked me for trying to help 'this potentially great country!' The lost decade of Jacob Zuma was brought to a close by an extraordinarily courageous press and judiciary and the most effective civil society I have ever seen operating anywhere.

I would dislike it to be thought that I spent all my time working in South Africa. In this sports-mad country, with its magnificent scenery, there were plenty of other ways to pass the time, fly-fishing with Helen Suzman being one of them. While I put back the fish, as a believer in taking no prisoners, she kept every one. When I caught a huge trout in Natal, my fly-fishing guru, Tom Sutcliffe, included this in his book, *Hunting Trout*, but did not fail to point out that my first cast had to be retrieved from the pullover of our fishing companion.

Every weekend in Cape Town, there was tennis with Alex Boraine, who, with Van Zyl Slabbert, was building bridges to the ANC and was to serve as the key organiser of Desmond Tutu's Truth and Reconciliation Commission. And occasionally with Gordon Forbes, author of the most entertaining book ever written about tennis, *A Handful of Summers*, describing his experiences on the still amateur tour as the room-mate of Rod Laver.

On a foray into the Okavango Delta with the Finance Minister, Barend du Plessis, and the head of the South African Foreign Ministry, Neil van Heerden, our passports were stamped by a grinning immigration officer who told us that he had just been listening on the radio to President Botha declaring that it was much too dangerous for South Africans to visit Botswana.

CHAPTER XXV

A SPECIALLY CLOSE RELATIONSHIP

On returning to Washington as British Ambassador in August 1991, my first effort was to seek to ban the use by anyone in the embassy of the term 'special relationship'.

This was not because I did not believe that the relationship was special – the nuclear, defence and intelligence cooperation undoubtedly is – but because the term had been so extensively abused by the political class and press in Britain that I wanted to hear it, if at all, from the Americans, and not from us.

Every Whitehall official or press commentator otherwise would continue to bemoan 'the end of the special relationship' every time the Americans disagreed with us, as they frequently did and were bound to do. I did so despite the fact that the relationship with George Bush Sr *was* pretty special and, contrary to many forecasts, was to become so with his successor.

I tried to persuade anyone willing to listen to start describing it as the 'specially close relationship' – a far more accurate description of what it actually is (on which please see Chapter XXIX).

* * *

My first task was to accompany the Prime Minister, John Major, on a visit to George Bush's holiday home in Kennebunkport in Maine – a wonderful opportunity to get to know the Bush team at first hand. The visit coincided with the attempt to overthrow Gorbachev in Moscow. Bush and Major condemned the coup and were mightily relieved when, thanks to Boris Yeltsin, it failed.

For me, this was the start of a firm friendship with General Brent Scowcroft, regarded by many, then and since, as America's best ever national security adviser. When the President and Prime Minister went fishing, Scowcroft forecast correctly that this would not cause any danger to the fish. Brent was famous for sleeping through Cabinet meetings, on the grounds that nothing of any importance ever happened in them.

When Saddam Hussein invaded Kuwait, there had been divided views in Washington about the response, with some tempted to limit US involvement to protecting Saudi Arabia. The President and Scowcroft had wanted to do more than that but, as Colin Powell reminded me, it was immediately after his meeting with Margaret Thatcher in Aspen that Bush had declared, 'This aggression will not stand,' causing Powell to accelerate the military preparations. When Bush telephoned her to say that the US (briefly) was suspending action against Iraqi ships, she famously had replied, 'All right, but this is no time to go wobbly, George!'

He genuinely admired her but was impatient with her reservations about German reunification. When he wrote to her to say that they must tie Germany into Europe, she replied that they might rather find that they had tied Europe to Germany.

I was not surprised, therefore, to find George Bush confiding to me, on this and other occasions, that he found John Major much easier to deal with than Margaret Thatcher, there being no doubt in their relationship who was the senior partner. He was appreciative of Major's firm support in the Gulf War and was both generous and protective towards him, deploring Thatcher's criticisms of her successor. He also was exceptionally kind to me, with frequent invitations to the White House, where he enjoyed showing us the scorch marks left behind by Admiral Cockburn when he and his marines set fire to the building in 1814. I periodically would receive short manuscript notes from the President, leaving me wondering how on earth he had time to do this.

George Bush's service to his country had started as the youngest US Navy pilot in the Pacific in World War II. He recounted to me how, after sixty missions, having been shot down by the Japanese, he found himself floating in a small yellow life vest with no hope of rescue until, miraculously, he was hauled on to the deck of a US submarine.

He was a true believer in the notion of the US as the 'indispensable nation', called upon to help others defend themselves against the threats they faced. With an unrivalled expertise in foreign affairs, he seemed barely interested in domestic policy. The contrast could not have been starker between his outstanding policy team and his warring and leaky domestic advisers. George Bush Jr, at the time manager of the Texas Rangers baseball team, used to tell me how appalled he was at the apparent lack of any discipline or loyalty among them.

George Bush had started 1991 with an approval rating of 90 per cent after his success in the Gulf War. But the very patrician, Yale-educated President was no orator. 'We are enjoying sluggish times, and not enjoying them very much,' he said on one occasion. In contrast to Reagan, he did not, as he said himself, do 'the vision thing'. He lacked his predecessor's ability to get through to ordinary

Americans. The key Reagan organiser in California, Stu Spencer, warned me that Bush was going to lose the state by a mile. 'I think he knows more about Kuwait than California.' The Reaganites, sidelined by the new President's team, started referring to them as 'country club Republicans'.

An extremely saddening early task for me was to take to the White House to see President Bush meet the families of the British soldiers who had been killed in a friendly fire incident in the Gulf War. George Bush displayed huge sympathy with and kindness to the grieving families, and casualties among our forces would have been far higher without US air cover, but there could have been no more bitter reminder of the real cost of war.

Saddam Hussein's defeat had led to an insurrection by the Kurds in northern Iraq. As Saddam was using his air force against them, the Prime Minister, John Major, called for the creation of a safe area, entailing establishment of a no-fly zone. As Colin Powell, with grim amusement, observed to me, the realities of power were that this amounted to a call on the US Air Force to enforce it! George Bush ruled that they should do so.

Alan Greenspan was one of my mentors in Washington. With Lou Preston, head of the World Bank, we used to have dinner together on Sunday evenings. But the Federal Reserve was slow to cut interest rates despite weakness in the economy. By Easter 1992, Jonathan Powell, first secretary in the embassy, and I were convinced that George Bush's victory in the November election was by no means assured. I agreed with Jonathan that he should attach himself to the campaign of the only Democratic candidate who looked to have competent political skills, the 'New Democrat' Governor of Arkansas, both of them being alumni of University College, Oxford. Jonathan started on the Clinton bus, before graduating to the Clinton plane, and becoming both a member and a favourite of the Clinton entourage.

Meanwhile, relations could not have been closer with Scowcroft and with Colin Powell, chairman of the joint chiefs of staff. I had been warned about the difficulty of getting face-time with the Secretary of State, James Baker. This problem, fortunately, was solved by a friend, owner of the Washington Redskins, who would install us together in his seats at all home games whenever Baker was in town.

I became a great admirer of Baker, a key architect of German reunification, and of his outstanding deputy, Bob Zoellick, subsequently head of the World Bank. At a time when the European Bureau of the State Department were expressing their dismay at Britain's failure to join the euro, Baker kept telling me, over a hot dog, that in his opinion, as a former Treasury Secretary, we would have to be crazy to do so.

Easter 1992 marked a turning point, when George Bush was reported to be considering and was being advised to drop the Vice-President, Dan Quayle, from the ticket for re-election and replace him with a more impressive running mate. Baker, who would have been by far the best candidate, supposedly was ruled out as both he and Bush came from Texas, but the names being canvassed included that of Colin Powell. Quayle hastened to seek from the President an assurance that, having been loyal, he would not be dropped, and George Bush did not have the heart to do so. Instead, Baker was moved from being Secretary of State, at which he excelled, back to the White House.

Baker was replaced as Secretary of State by an old friend from the Falklands War, Larry Eagleburger. Hearing that the consular division of the State Department was about to issue a statement warning Americans not to travel to Northern Ireland, I asked to see him about this. Having armed myself with the relevant crime statistics, I pointed out that it was twenty times more dangerous to visit Washington DC. Did the US really want us to have to point this out? Amidst guffaws from Larry, the warning about Northern Ireland was abandoned.

Having returned as chief of staff in the White House, I found Jim Baker far from optimistic about the election. With the economy still weak, as he travelled around the country, he was getting a bad feeling. The maverick independent candidate Ross Perot, campaigning against the North American Free Trade Area (NAFTA), was syphoning away a lot of votes.

Tasked with writing a speech for him, Bob Zoellick asked George Bush what message he wanted to get across. That he would do a better job than the other guy was the reply, leaving Zoellick dismayed at the lack of vision this implied. When it came to the presidential debates, the former navy pilot George Bush was too much of a gentleman to ask the question the Clinton camp had been dreading: 'What makes you think you are qualified to be commander in chief?'

At this stage I took Margaret Thatcher, who was staying at the embassy, to see President Bush in the Oval Office. Instead of the usual pleasantries, her opening salvo was, 'George, why on earth don't you change your position against abortion?' All Republican candidates were required to toe this line, but she knew he didn't believe in it. The President replied feebly that his pollster had assured him that it was only the seventeenth most important issue. There followed a 'You just don't understand' exchange, in which she said that for many younger women it was *the* most important issue. As Baker observed to me afterwards, she was absolutely right.

The truth was that George Bush was a great public servant rather than a political animal, whereas his opponent was a political animal to his very core. He simply could not believe that the American people would end up voting for someone manifestly less honourable than him. Thanks to the impact of the campaign of Ross Perot, Bill Clinton was able to win the election with just 43 per cent of the votes.

John Major appeared for a final meeting in the Bush presidency, at which the President nearly broke down as he spoke about the election outcome. Two days before leaving the White House, he invited us to a final dinner there with his staff. A kinder and more generous man was not to be found among world leaders. It had been a privilege to work with James Baker, Brent Scowcroft, Colin Powell and Larry Eagleburger, who together represented the most impressive foreign policy team since Dean Acheson and George Marshall. The contrast could not have been greater with the initial confusion and hesitancy of Bill Clinton's foreign policy.

George Bush was a one-term President. But historians will not fail to conclude that in managing the end of the Cold War, the reunification of Germany and the reduction of nuclear weapons, plus the liberation of Kuwait, he made a greater and more positive impact on world affairs than any of his successors has done. Bill Clinton was not a bad President, better attuned to dealing with all the domestic policy issues. Yet it was with real sadness that we said goodbye to George Bush. For in purely human terms, it was difficult to feel that the better man had won. Bush's experience and that of his colleagues were to be badly missed as the west tried and for three years largely failed to deal with the crisis in the former Yugoslavia.

CHAPTER XXVI

GETTING TO KNOW
THE CLINTONS

R elations with the new administration began with a
comedy of errors. Republican staffers had been trying
to discover if Bill Clinton had applied for British citizenship
in attempting to avoid being drafted to Vietnam during his
studies at Oxford. In an attempt to kill the story, a Home
Office spokesman declared that there was no trace of this –
thereby suggesting that the files had been examined.

My own inside information about Clinton at Oxford
was confined to an exchange with Germaine Greer, who,
addressing the Oxford Union, had declared that she was
no longer interested in middle-class intellectuals: only
blue-collar workers would do. According to a Clinton
classmate, a voice from the back of the hall had responded, 'But Miss Greer, won't you give us one last chance?'

But Douglas Hurd had wished James Baker 'good hunting' in the election. A couple of Tories had tried to help the

Republican campaign. The Clinton staffer and conspiracy theorist Sidney Blumenthal was convinced the Conservatives had been plotting with the Republicans against the Clintons. It certainly was true that the Major government would greatly have preferred George Bush to win.

It was the embassy's job to anticipate a possible change, to keep in touch with the leading Democrat foreign policy experts, several of whom were personal friends, and thereby to contain any resultant damage. While Jonathan Powell had become almost a part of the Clinton team, I had several meetings with those we believed were likely to occupy the key foreign policy posts in the new administration: Warren Christopher, Strobe Talbott, Tony Lake and Richard Holbrooke.

When Bill Clinton visited Washington briefly before his inauguration, Kay Graham, owner of the *Washington Post* and *Newsweek*, gave a dinner for him, to which we were the only non-Americans invited, and ensured that I had some time with the President elect. I asked him to look beyond the press claims about Tory support for the Republicans in the election. He would need support in dealing with Saddam Hussein. He would find John Major a key ally in doing so and should see him as soon as possible after the inauguration, which he agreed to do.

There was an argument over dinner, to the amusement of others, with my future neighbour, the Vice-President elect,

Al Gore. He cheerfully agreed to abandon Dan Quayle's habit of taking off in a helicopter to go and play golf at the Congressional Club seven miles away, but launched into an attack on us for appeasing the Serbs in Bosnia. I said that we would take the US seriously on the subject when they agreed to commit some forces there, as we had done.

When John Major arrived for his first encounter with the new President, the meeting was friendly and went according to plan, but with no great personal chemistry. Temperamentally, they could hardly have been more different.

Clinton had appointed as his Treasury Secretary our close friend in the Senate, Lloyd Bentsen. Bentsen had brought some Texan habits with him to Washington. As his socialite wife proved reluctant to leave parties, he would seize her in a fireman's lift and walk out with her over his shoulder. With Robert Rubin, Laura Tyson and for a while Roger Altman, this was an extremely impressive economic team. They persuaded Clinton in his first budget to raise taxes to narrow the budget deficit, with positive economic results, but contributing to a surge against the Democrats in the midterm elections.

The suspicions in the Clinton camp about the Conservative government did not apply to the embassy. We were invited to dinner by the Clintons shortly after their arrival in the White House, with Hillary telling me excitedly about her plans for healthcare reform. In personal terms, both proved every bit as friendly and approachable as George and Barbara Bush. I gave a return dinner for their staff and advisers, led by Madeleine Albright, several of whom seemed barely out of college and blissfully unaware of the realities they would face in dealing with Congress. Hillary herself mistook the applause for her presentation on healthcare as a sign that hard-bitten Senators actually would support her 1,000-page bill, despite the lack of clarity as to how it would be funded, and found it a searing experience when they did not.

Bill Clinton, who had appointed no fewer than twenty-three Rhodes scholars to his administration, including the future Deputy Secretary of State, Strobe Talbott, attended a celebratory reception at the embassy. In Los Angeles I had met Barbra Streisand, who tackled me about Northern Ireland, as did Paul Newman, who was supporting mixed Catholic and Protestant youth projects. A summons by Streisand to her concert in Washington led to an evening with the President schmoozing the star, to the foot-tapping displeasure of Hillary.

As his Secretary for Defense, Clinton had appointed a Washington friend of mine, Congressman Les Aspin. Much as I liked Les, the appointment alarmed me, as, though a genuine defence intellectual, he was completely disorganised. Soon, the corridor outside the Defense Secretary's office in the Pentagon was filled with generals and admirals queueing up for meetings that started hours late.

CHAPTER XXVII

TOWARDS A PEACE IN NORTHERN IRELAND

In my previous term in Washington, under the Reagan administration, relations with the US government over Northern Ireland had been straightforward. Judge Bill Webster, head of the FBI, told me that it was not within their power to prevent fundraising for the IRA in the pubs of Boston and San Francisco, but by tying the organisers up in constant lawsuits, they could ensure that most of the proceeds stayed in the US. Rudy Giuliani, at the time the prosecuting attorney in New York, also showed particular zeal in chasing fundraisers for the IRA.

On my return to Washington as Ambassador, I found that our consular staff in Boston and New York had done a first-class job in maintaining extremely close contact with the moderate leaders of the Irish American community.

In my first meeting with Teddy Kennedy, undisputed leader on Irish affairs in the Senate, I argued that a future peace in Northern Ireland was going to depend critically on the emergence of new leaders within the Protestant community. The old-guard unionists like Ian Paisley and Jim Molyneux had long since given up on Congress as hopelessly biased against them. If I could persuade the more forward-looking unionist leaders to make the effort, would Kennedy guarantee me that they would get a fair hearing?

As a gesture to the Kennedys and to the Irish American community, Bill Clinton had appointed Teddy Kennedy's sister, Jean Kennedy Smith, as the US Ambassador in Dublin. She proved incapable of seeing Ireland, north and south, except in shades of green. The Irish Ambassador told me that on arrival in Dublin she had greeted with disbelief the discovery that the Irish government did not want reunification without the consent of the majority of the people of Northern Ireland, as that would saddle them with an incipient civil war.

Despite the portrayal of him by the British tabloids, this was not the view of Teddy Kennedy. Both he and his staff, however, were pretty well joined at the hip to the moderate Catholic leader John Hume, a constant visitor to Washington and the US, with on their part virtually no contact with and little understanding of the unionists. Nevertheless, Kennedy undertook to give Ken Maginnis and others a fair hearing, a promise that he kept.

I had been on friendly terms with John Hume since getting

him invited to visit Brussels by the European Commission. Not entirely to my surprise, he found the euro briefings rather boring and the Commission told me that he disappeared one evening, only to return next morning with one sleeve of his jacket missing. But he was absolutely sincere in his quest for peace in Northern Ireland, though his views naturally were from the perspective of the Catholic community.

There followed quite a surprise as, via the Consul, I received an invitation from Tom O'Neill, son of the former Speaker Tip O'Neill, to attend the annual St Patrick's Day dinner in Boston. I thought it wise to check with Kennedy and with Mayor Flynn that this really was intended, which they said it was.

So I turned up at their flagship dinner in the Irish American heartland. The introductions began with the O'Neills (huge applause), Mayor Flynn (huge applause), the Irish Ambassador (warm applause), then the British Ambassador (audible gasp from the 1,000-strong attendance). Having survived that initiation, I got a friendly reception and the dinner raised a million dollars for worthwhile causes on both sides of the border.

* * *

By this time, the current Speaker, Tom Foley, was warning me that moves were afoot to try to get a visa to enable

Gerry Adams, leader of Sinn Féin and joined at the hip to the IRA, to visit Washington. Foley was strongly opposed to this, as were the State Department.

John Hume, however, had managed to convince Teddy Kennedy and his former aide, now on the National Security Council staff, that this could help towards a political settlement in Northern Ireland. I made clear, among others to the Vice-President, Al Gore, that given the US and British positions on terrorism, it would be a travesty to give Adams a visa unless he dissociated himself completely from IRA violence, a message also conveyed direct from No. 10 to Clinton. There followed a meeting between Adams and the US Consul General in Belfast in which Adams declined to do so, leading the Consul General and the State Department to advise against admitting him.

As Kennedy continued to lobby, when I met Clinton at a dinner attended also by Tom Foley, he was so evasive that it was clear to both of us that he intended to grant the visa, now being recommended also by the National Security Adviser, Tony Lake. The Prime Minister, John Major, with good reason, was so furious that he refused to take calls from Clinton for several days.

I was just as annoyed at the decision to issue the visa without any undertakings from Adams, but, as I pointed out to Lake and others in the White House, if they did not now help to deliver an IRA ceasefire, they would be left looking very foolish indeed. They needed no convincing of this and intense pressure was applied to Adams to help to deliver one.

This episode was followed by one of John Hume's regular visits to the embassy, in the course of which a bottle of Scotch would disappear, not much of it inside me. My friend was more than usually conspiratorial. In hushed tones he told me that 'the boys' had decided to call off the armed struggle. This was for real, he contended, because it came from the 'hard man', Martin McGuinness, rather than from Adams. The same message, some time before, had gone direct from the IRA to No. 10.

A new St Patrick's Day celebration approached, this time at the White House. The Northern Ireland Secretary, Sir Patrick Mayhew, and others were invited. It was decided that the first ever meeting between Adams and a British Cabinet minister should be held, as discreetly as possible, in Washington. We arranged this on neutral ground at the Shoreham Hotel. Patrick Mayhew was panicky that he might somehow be photographed shaking Adams's hand or have it reported that he had done so. To try to reassure him, I pointed out that while this might mean the end of his political career, for Adams it could entail being shot by one of his own supporters.

The meeting took place without incident, in an

atmosphere of extreme wariness. But this small step led on to others. A negotiating process had begun.

The Northern Ireland Office had continued to worry about any US involvement at all, but I did not feel that our record in Northern Ireland had been so stellar that we could afford to dispense with any external support, provided it was channelled in the right way. We had made very clear to the Clinton White House that there must be no involvement whatever in our negotiations with the parties. If they wanted to show support, this should be by opening up the prospect of US investment, which the Commerce Secretary, Ron Brown, duly was asked to do.

When Brown was killed in an air crash in 1996, the mantle of acting as a kind of Dutch uncle to the participants in the negotiations passed to George Mitchell, well known to us as the extremely astute former majority leader in the Senate. An inspired choice by Clinton, George Mitchell seemed instinctively to understand all the prejudices, including our own, and ended up making a real contribution to peace in Northern Ireland.

Behind this lay a transformation in the attitude of Bill Clinton. The original decision to grant a visa to Adams had been taken primarily for domestic political reasons. But as this drama unfolded, Clinton became intensely interested in Northern Ireland, down to the last detail. He also developed an admiration for the dogged determination with which, amidst the myriad difficulties, the Prime Minister was pursuing the chance of peace in the province. There was between them none of the easy relationship with his soulmate Tony Blair, but Clinton ended up confessing to me that he had underestimated John Major.

So what had started out as an intervention regarded as very unhelpful in the affairs of Northern Ireland ended up as an essentially positive one. The NSC staff remained much better at understanding the Sinn Féin point of view than that of the unionists, which they scarcely bothered to understand at all. But this didn't matter, as Clinton, having become so engaged, could be relied upon to deliver the messages he was asked to send to the Catholic political leaders.

The role of the embassy was marginal. But not that of a key component of it. When, early in 1994, Tony Blair visited Washington with Gordon Brown, I had asked Jonathan Powell to organise their programme. When Blair was elected leader of the Labour Party, it came as no surprise when Jonathan told me that he had been asked to become Blair's chief of staff. I encouraged him to accept, as it was pretty clear by then that Blair was going to be the next Prime Minister and he would be in much need of that kind of support.

This, ironically, was strikingly close to the role his brother Charles had played with Margaret Thatcher, though

Jonathan managed to keep a lower profile. Though he accepted Gordon Brown's five economic tests for joining the euro, Blair was more euro-positive than the Chancellor and from time to time was urged by Peter Mandelson, by then our Commissioner in Brussels, to reopen joining it. I was asked by No. 10 whether opinion in the City was warming towards joining. Regarding this as bad politics and worse economics, I poured what cold water I could on these dreams.

Jonathan played a vital role, along with others, in keeping the peace negotiations on track and managing US involvement in the process. He since has played an important role in the peace talks with the Basque separatists in Spain and with the FARC guerrillas in Colombia.

As the time came to leave Washington, I received a handwritten note from Teddy Kennedy thanking me for my role in supporting peace in Northern Ireland, which had been extremely modest, and summoning me to a ceremony he wanted us to conduct together outside the Senate. On arrival, I was greeted by the Senator plus aides carrying a shovel and a small tree. We were going to plant this, the Senator announced to the paparazzi, as a new Liberty Tree, to make up for the one we had cut down in Boston during the Revolutionary Wars!

CHAPTER XXVIII

'WE DO NOT HAVE A DOG
IN THIS FIGHT'

In Bosnia, with the best of intentions, we had sent forces on, initially, a humanitarian mission, which quickly morphed into an attempted peace-keeping mission. In a meeting with Henry Kissinger soon after my return to Washington, we both felt that a huge opportunity had been missed when the Serbs were shelling the Croat enclave of Dubrovnik. An air strike on the Serb artillery positions would have put a rapid end to behaviour of this kind.

But the Bush administration, heading for an election, was engaged in bringing half a million men back from the Gulf. They had no desire to become enmeshed in the Balkans, with Baker allegedly declaring, 'We do not have a dog in this fight.' It was left to the Europeans to resolve this quarrel on their doorstep, with the Luxembourg Foreign Minister, Jacques Poos, announcing on behalf of the European Community that this was 'the hour of Europe'.

As the crisis developed, I found myself reflecting on two famous sayings, neither of them authentic but both true. The first was attributed, including by John Kennedy, to Edmund Burke: 'For evil to triumph, it is sufficient for good men to do nothing.' This is nowhere to be found in his writings. It should be attributed instead to John Stuart Mill, who declared, 'Bad men need nothing more to encompass their ends, than that good men should look on and do nothing.'

As we persisted in an attempted peace-keeping operation in the absence of a peace to keep, the other thought that sprang to mind was that, supposedly, of Einstein: 'The definition of insanity is doing the same thing over and over again and expecting a different result.' This too is nowhere to be found in his writings, but nevertheless applied to our efforts in Bosnia. We could and should have ended this conflict much sooner than we did.

By the end of the Bush administration, Larry Eagleburger was telling me that he thought the Serbs should be given an ultimatum about their aggression in Bosnia, only for him by then to be timed out.

When the Clinton administration arrived, it was highly critical of the European efforts to contain the fighting in Bosnia, to the irritation of the chief European negotiator, David Owen, who in turn told his friend Johnny Apple of the *New York Times* what he thought of their performance. In reality, at this time, Bill Clinton had no intention of getting involved. His priorities were entirely domestic. Hillary, he told me, had given him a copy of *Balkan Ghosts* by Robert Kaplan, chronicling the 1,000-year history of mayhem in the Balkans. I found him trying to quote to me Bismarck's dictum about the whole of the Balkans not being worth the bones of a single Pomeranian grenadier.

In October 1992, I attended a meeting with the Prime Minister in London. There was nervousness in Whitehall about the proposal to declare a military no-fly zone over Bosnia to prevent the Yugoslav Air Force being used by their Bosnian Serb allies to attack the Bosnian Muslims. This, it was feared, would be an escalation. I said that the Americans were confident that this could be enforced without firing a shot, as the Yugoslav Air Force were unlikely to try to intervene in the certainty of being shot down – a prediction that turned out to be correct.

In May 1993, the Secretary of State, Warren Christopher, was despatched to Europe, ostensibly to win the Europeans over to a policy of lifting the arms embargo and launching air strikes on the Serbs. While Christopher was on his plane across the Atlantic, the US Defense Secretary, Les Aspin, rang me to say that the Pentagon did not really agree with this, in particular with lifting the arms embargo. It was, he suggested, up to the British to help to 'save us from ourselves'. There was a clear hint of what I knew already: that the President did not really want the US to get involved.

In his meeting at Chevening with John Major, Douglas Hurd and the Defence Secretary, Malcolm Rifkind, Christopher was accompanied by the US Ambassador in London, my close friend Ray Seitz. A George Bush Sr appointee, previously the number two in London and the first career diplomat to be appointed as US Ambassador there in living memory, Seitz had become a trusted figure with the British political establishment. Seitz, furthermore, used to claim that if he and I swapped positions, no one would notice the difference.

As he told me at the time, and wrote subsequently in his engaging memoir, *Over Here* (in which he contends that what the British are best at are dogs and gardens), the lawyerly, cautious and utterly uncharismatic Warren Christopher argued the case for lifting the arms embargo and launching air strikes against the Serbs 'with all the verve of a solicitor going over a conveyancing deed'. The British side rejected 'lift and strike' as, in our opinion, unworkable and a threat to the British forces on the ground.

The Pentagon agreed that lifting the arms embargo would risk intensifying Serb attacks before the Muslims could be provided with heavy weapons and trained to use them. But they had far more confidence than their British counterparts that the use of air power could be decisive against the Serbs. With what I knew of US technology and their development of precision-guided weapons, I felt pretty sure they were right. Clearly, however, it was not going to be possible to find out until the US really was prepared to exercise decisive leadership and a plan existed to withdraw to greater safety the scattered British forces on the ground.

In debates with Senator John McCain and others on the Ted Koppel and Jim Lehrer programmes, I found that most Americans were fair-minded enough to accept that it was of little use criticising unless they were prepared to get directly involved themselves.

In February 1994, the shelling of the marketplace in Sarajevo appeared to offer the opportunity to deal far more decisively with the Serbs. They were confronted for the first time with a NATO-backed ultimatum, not yet another warning from the hapless UN representative Yasushi Akashi, requiring them to withdraw all their artillery more than twenty miles from Sarajevo.

As the Serbs failed to comply with this demand, the US Air Force were expecting, with the French and the RAF, to take action against them. But the UN commander, General Sir Michael Rose, certified that the Serb guns within the exclusion zone were now all under UN control. Facing great difficulties at the time, with the Bosnians mounting small-scale attacks that brought a crushing response from the Serbs, Rose was indignant at being second-guessed by the Americans from afar.

This produced an explosion from the normally imperturbable General Shalikashvili, who had succeeded Colin Powell as chairman of the joint chiefs of staff. We had, he told me, just made a very grave mistake. The Serbs had been allowed blatantly to defy a NATO ultimatum. Their heavy weapons remaining within the exclusion zone should have been destroyed in air strikes. Furthermore, it was simply not true that they had been brought under UN control. Pretty soon they would be firing again on Sarajevo.

Late in 1994, there was a positive development as Richard Holbrooke returned from his post as US Ambassador in Bonn to become Assistant Secretary for European affairs. The hard-charging, arrogant and supposedly 'difficult' Holbrooke had been a friend since my previous tour in Washington. He was determined to bring a new energy to US policy in the Balkans and I was no less determined to help him.

In January 1995, General Rupert Smith was appointed to take over command of the UN Protection Force in Bosnia. Smith had distinguished himself as commander of the British armoured division in the liberation of Kuwait. As he visited Washington before taking up his post, he appeared far more resolute about standing up to the Serbs than his predecessors had been.

Shalikashvili's prediction had proved to be true. The Serb artillery that had not been removed from the exclusion zone continued to be used to bombard Sarajevo. The UN-designated supposedly 'safe areas' were regularly being shelled by the Serbs. Limited actions against them simply resulted in British and other members of the UN force in their scattered locations being taken hostage by them.

The position of the UN force by this stage had become so precarious that I was instructed to tell General Shalikashvili that we might have to withdraw. If we did, extricating our forces in the midst of the civil war could be very hazardous. We might have to ask for US help in getting them out. Shalikashvili said that, if it came to that and we needed help, e.g. from a US airborne division, he would recommend that we should get it. But he would have to consult the President.

This was the moment at which General Mladić commanded personally the Bosnian Serb attack on the Muslim enclave of Srebrenica, protected by a battalion of Dutch peacekeepers. The enclave was rapidly overrun, with the UN peacekeepers powerless to prevent the subsequent massacre of 8,000 male inhabitants of Srebrenica.

The enclave of Goražde, protected by a small force of British peacekeepers, very clearly was next in line.

I was by now within a few weeks of ending my tour in Washington. I had been fortunate to establish a very friendly relationship with President Clinton. Through his chief of staff, Mack McLarty, very exceptionally, I asked to see the President on his own. Once in the Oval Office, I said that if the Serbs were permitted to do in Goražde and potentially Sarajevo what they had done in Srebrenica, I did not believe that the reputation of any western leader would survive. To my relief, I found that Bill Clinton had reached this conclusion himself. The national security adviser, Tony Lake, joined in the last few minutes of the meeting.

The crisis brought Malcolm Rifkind, who had taken over from Douglas Hurd as Foreign Secretary, post-haste to Washington. On his arrival, I told him that he would find that the US would support the delivery of an ultimatum to General Mladić, not from the UN, but from the head of US Strike Command and his British and French counterparts.

The ultimatum duly was delivered to Mladić by the US Air Force commander, in black leather jacket and dark glasses, the head of RAF Strike Command, and their French counterpart, warning Mladić what would happen if there were an attack in particular on Goražde or other 'safe areas'. I was pleased to get a first-hand account of this long-overdue confrontation with Mladić from David

Omand of the Ministry of Defence, who attended this encounter with him.

By this stage, the facts on the ground in Bosnia were changing rapidly as a result of a successful Croat offensive to regain ground they had lost to the over-extended Serbs.

There followed an utterly unnecessary tragedy. Holbrooke's deputy, Robert Frasure, had been a friend since we had served at the same time in South Africa. As Bob had exposed covert South African military activities in Angola and Mozambique, his family had been terrorised by the dirty tricks division of South African military intelligence to an extent that led to him having to be withdrawn.

As Holbrooke sought to engage with the Bosnian parties, his deputy, Frasure, and two colleagues, visiting the front lines near Sarajevo, were prevented by the Bosnian Serbs from using the only safe route out of the area. Instead, on 19 August 1995, they had to travel along a track around the precipitous slopes of Mount Igman. The armoured vehicle in which they were travelling slipped off the track and crashed, killing Frasure and his colleagues.

With President Clinton, Richard Holbrooke and his stricken family, I attended the sombre ceremony at Andrews air force base as the bodies were returned from Bosnia. The tragedy, they both made clear, had increased their determination to deal decisively with the underlying problem.

As I left Washington, on 28 August 1995 the Serbs shelled the marketplace in Sarajevo, killing over forty people. The new British Defence Secretary, Michael Portillo, had approved General Rupert Smith's plan to withdraw the British contingent from Goražde in preparation for serious NATO action against the Serbs. The air campaign began on 30 August, lasting until 20 September, with a bombardment by the US Air Force, supported by the RAF and the French, against targets they had been working on for months. Thanks to the accuracy of the targeting, predictions that the Serbs could not be deterred by the use of air power were confounded.

The bombardment paved the way for the negotiations led by Richard Holbrooke in Dayton, Ohio, that resulted in the peace that prevails in Sarajevo today. At a crucial point in those talks, Holbrooke escorted the Serb Premier, Slobodan Milošević, on whose support the Bosnian Serbs depended, through the massive Wright-Patterson air force base hangar containing the full panoply of US air power, a demonstration that had its effect on Milošević. The crisis that had threatened at times to inflict permanent damage on the North Atlantic alliance had culminated at last in decisive NATO action to bring it to an end.

* * *

In May 1994, I had accompanied the then Defence Secretary, Malcolm Rifkind, to Cape Canaveral to board the British nuclear submarine HMS *Vanguard* for the test firing of the first UK Trident missile. The massive submarine sailed out to sea pursued by a flotilla of Greenpeace vessels determined to prevent the test firing taking place. Until quite late afternoon they succeeded, as we could not release the missile with any of the small Greenpeace vessels in periscope view.

The US admiral accompanying us regaled us with the story of what had happened when Greenpeace had tried this on him. Knowing what to expect, he had arranged for speedboats to cover the Greenpeace vessels with foam, rendering it impossible for their occupants to stand up. Their propellers had been enmeshed in wire. As a finale, a US destroyer had 'nudged' the Greenpeace mothership out of the way. For this, the US Navy were fined half a million dollars. 'Worth every goddam cent', in the feisty admiral's view. The Defence Secretary listened with alarm to this account, which, we explained, was not an option for our test.

Once we had dived deep and far enough to lose Greenpeace and climbed back towards the surface, the huge ship shuddered as the missile was released. Through the television monitor as it left the hull, it appeared initially to lift incredibly slowly off the submarine until it soared off into space, before landing in the designated area in the Indian Ocean.

On the way back, we watched *Mutiny on the Bounty*.

A decade before, following a visit to the Rand Corporation on the west coast, I had informed the Ministry of Defence about the first US tests of the Tomahawk missile, which, they claimed, could be fired from a couple of hundred miles away, 'but still fly through your garage door'.

As Saddam Hussein, despite his crushing defeat, was still in power and intent on crushing his domestic enemies, we had to look for ways of deterring him. As he blocked inspection of suspect military sites, Colin Powell informed me that the US intended to retaliate against the military and intelligence headquarters in Baghdad. Seventeen Cruise missiles were fired, all finding their targets, except for one, which landed instead in the foyer of the hotel where most of the western journalists were staying, killing the receptionist.

As I left Washington, the Americans decided to ban flights by Saddam's military aircraft south as well as north of Baghdad. As I had been suggesting this for some time, Tony Lake, Clinton's national security adviser, claimed that this was to be known as the Renwick memorial project. The containment of Saddam Hussein was working. The Prime Minister announced the acquisition for our own armed forces of a number of Tomahawk missiles to give them the ability in case of need to attack hostile targets without imperilling RAF aircrew.

* * *

Colin Powell had been recommended for an honorary knighthood in recognition of his services to the allies in the Gulf War. After the ceremony at Buckingham Palace, his namesake, colleague and great friend Charles Powell gave a dinner in his honour. Colin told me gleefully that Charles had declared that in the Powell family, the tradition was that the first son inherited the estate, the second went into the armed forces and the third into the church, while the black sheep of the family went off to the colonies. It was, he claimed, a great pleasure to welcome the black sheep back again.

As Colin observed, this was not a speech that could possibly have been made in the United States.

CHAPTER XXIX

FIGHTING WITH ALLIES

On leaving Washington, I published on both sides of the Atlantic an account of the at times real, at others so-called special relationship since its inception in the desperate summer of 1940. The purpose was to seek to demystify and describe the rollercoaster nature of the relationship not on the basis of my opinions, but through the eyes and reminiscences of the principal actors on both sides.

It began with an episode much less well remembered in Britain than in the United States. This was the capture of Washington by Admiral Cockburn and his marines in 1814. As President Madison escaped across the Potomac in a rowing boat, Cockburn found the table set for the President's dinner, which he ate before burning down the White House and the other public buildings in Washington and making about First Lady Dolley Madison 'pleasantries too vulgar to repeat'.

As Cockburn sailed on to bombard Fort McHenry, Francis Scott Key next morning saw that 'our flag was still there', giving the fledgling nation its national anthem.

Relations were little better throughout the rest of the nineteenth century. In 1860, the British minister was unimpressed by the Republican candidate in the presidential election, 'a Mr Lincoln, a man unknown, a rough westerner, of the lowest origin and little education'. This about the author of the Gettysburg Address.

By the end of the First World War, the United States had two million men under arms in Europe, but US forces did not participate in the fighting on the Western Front until April 1918, when the Ludendorff offensive caused the British commander in chief, Field Marshal Haig, to issue his desperate 'backs to the wall' order of the day. In the 1930s, the head of the Foreign Office, Sir Robert Vansittart, despairing of ever getting any help from the Americans in dealing with the European dictators, concluded that they 'will always let us down'. To win the 1940 presidential election, Franklin Roosevelt had to promise that 'your boys are not going to be sent into any foreign wars'.

For all his magnificent rhetoric, Churchill knew that the war against Hitler was not actually winnable without the US directly involved in it.

Following the Japanese attack on Pearl Harbor,

Churchill spent three weeks in the White House. According to Harry Hopkins, as Roosevelt wheeled himself into the Lincoln bedroom, he encountered Churchill emerging naked from his bath. As he hurriedly withdrew, Churchill is supposed to have said, 'No, Mr President, the Prime Minister of Great Britain has no secrets from the President of the United States.'*

None of which prevented violent disagreements about strategy. When the British defence chief Field Marshal Alan Brooke asked General George Marshall why the US wanted to try to invade France in 1943, Marshall said, 'Because it's the quickest way to end the war.' 'Yes, but not the way we want to,' was Alanbrooke's reply.

In 1944–45, Churchill was driven to distraction by the failure of Roosevelt and Eisenhower to understand Stalin's intentions, based on Roosevelt's conviction that, without Churchill, he could get on fine with 'Uncle Joe', in whom he detected a 'stalwart good humour', leading Churchill to conclude, 'The only thing worse than fighting with allies is having to fight without them.'

The war over, Truman interrupted nuclear cooperation with Britain (restored by Eisenhower) and insisted on unrestricted Jewish emigration to Palestine, without

---

* As Churchill observed, this was not strictly true. Having revealed to Roosevelt Britain's success in breaking German cyphers, he admitted intercepting US cypher traffic too, asking Roosevelt to destroy his letter to him about this. He also claimed always to have had a towel around his waist!

consulting the British, who were administering the territory. Anthony Eden told straightforward lies to the Americans about the Suez fiasco.

When Kennedy was elected President, Harold Macmillan wondered how he could get on with this 'cocky young
Irishman'. Following a brutal meeting with Khrushchev
in Vienna, a shaken Kennedy arrived in London. Over
drinks with Macmillan, Kennedy complained about the
press, including attacks on Jackie for spending too much
on clothes and refurbishing the White House. Macmillan asked why he bothered about this. Kennedy said that
surely he would be upset if they attacked his wife: what if
they suggested Lady Dorothy was a drunk? 'I would say,'
said Macmillan, 'I would say, you should have seen her
mother.'

The cancellation of the Skybolt missile, crucial for the
British nuclear deterrent, then caused a huge political
problem for Macmillan. Kennedy bailed him out by offering the Polaris submarine system instead, which most of
the press at the time failed to recognise was a far superior
offer to Skybolt.

There was no real rapport at all between Lyndon Johnson and Harold Wilson, with Johnson outraged that
Wilson would not contribute even 'a platoon of bagpipers'
to support the Americans in Vietnam; nor was there any
between Richard Nixon and Ted Heath. Heath saw the

negotiation of Britain's entry to the European Economic Community as the great achievement of his career. To the amazement of Henry Kissinger, he positively wanted to undo the specially close relationship with the United States and not to be treated as a specially close and trusted ally.

Margaret Thatcher knew that without US support, we could not recover the Falklands. But she did not appreciate Al Haig's efforts to arrange a 'disguised transfer of sovereignty' to Argentina. Reagan, from his innate sense of chivalry, was far more deferential to her than he would have been to any male Prime Minister. None of which prevented George Bush Sr and James Baker considering that she was 'just plain wrong' about German reunification and George Shultz saying the same about her reaction to the US invasion of Grenada.

The relationship always has been more important to Britain than to the United States. It never has been plain sailing. Nor can it ever be taken for granted. It has endured not because of sentiment, but due to common interests – economic and in defence and security. The United States is by far the largest investor in the United Kingdom; the UK is the largest investor in the US. Many in the political class and media in Britain to this day like to believe that we are somehow wiser and, 200 years after the Declaration of Independence, more experienced than the Americans, a view regarded as risible on the other side of the Atlantic, given the examples of folly on our own side – such as Suez and triggering Brexit with no clear idea what the outcome will be.

* * *

This was a period in which a far greater degree of bipartisanship existed in the United States and, in foreign policy at least, in Britain. Many Senators had strong cross-party friendships. The southern 'Dixie' Democrats supported Ronald Reagan, before becoming Republicans themselves. The NAFTA agreement was pushed through by Clinton with Republican support. Moderate Republicans like Nancy Kassebaum and John Chafee had more in common with moderate Democrats across the aisle than with Republican ultras like Jesse Helms.

One of the most closely guarded secrets in Washington is the existence of a tennis court, hidden deep inside the Senate's Russell Building. My partners there included Dan Coats, currently head of the US intelligence community. Each year a bipartisan group of Senators would migrate to the John Gardiner tennis ranch in Arizona during the recess. If not a more civilised, this was a far more collegiate era than exists in US politics today.

The Speaker Tip O'Neill talked to me admiringly of

Reagan's political skills. Each time he opposed the President, Reagan would use his weekly broadcast to the nationwide local radio stations to get his listeners to deliver a truckload of correspondence to the Speaker, telling him to desist. In foreign policy, too, a number of leading Democrats, including Al Gore, supported the war to liberate Kuwait.

The fiercely independent Republican John McCain, a good friend and ally of ours in the Senate, wanted to nominate a moderate Democrat, Joe Lieberman, as his running mate in the 2008 presidential election! The party hierarchy were appalled, but Lieberman would have been far more credible than his fall-back choice of Sarah Palin.

CHAPTER XXX

'NEVER FORGET THAT WE ARE NOT ON YOUR SIDE'

This alarming advice was given to me by one of my closest friends in the press, who went on to say that neither his editor nor, in his opinion, most of his readers, were interested in good news about officialdom. They preferred tales of pomposity and calamity, incompetence and spectacular own goals.

I thought of a couple of my predecessors in Washington who had suffered at the hands of the media. Lord Halifax was despatched there by Churchill, to get him out of the War Cabinet. He confessed to his friend King George VI that he did not really like Americans: 'In the mass, I have always found them dreadful.' Invited to watch a baseball game in Chicago, he was offered a hot dog, which he found not much to his taste. The press next day published photos of the Ambassador, instead of eating it, trying to dispose of it under his seat.

Sir Oliver Franks, friend of Dean Acheson, was asked by the local radio station what he would like for Christmas. Touched by this enquiry, he made a suitably modest request. On Christmas Day, listeners heard the Soviet Ambassador declaring that what he wanted for Christmas was peaceful co-existence. The French Ambassador opted for liberty and fraternity. This was followed by the polite voice of Sir Oliver Franks asking for a small box of candied fruit.

But my friend's advice proved to be misplaced. I had a lot of fun in my foreign service career, much of it with friends in the press. Staying with us in Delhi, James Cameron introduced me to the concept of the heart starter, insisting on a huge glass of brandy being served with his breakfast. He had just made a TV programme contending that aircraft carriers were a fiendishly expensive waste of money. The captain of the *Ark Royal* protested mildly that they might come in handy in some future conflict, but James was unconvinced.

The contingent in Rhodesia of hard-boiled Africa correspondents included Chris Munnion, author of *Banana Sunday*, Michael Holman, James MacManus and Martin Meredith. There was never any hope of pulling the wool over their eyes.

I did find it necessary, occasionally, to stonewall with my friends. When I asked Kieran Prendergast, the Governor's spokesman in Rhodesia, to do so for several days, amidst tense exchanges with General Walls and Mugabe, an American correspondent sneeringly observed that Ron Ziegler (Nixon's spokesman) was alive and well and living in Harare. As Kieran stepped down from the podium with a view to punching him, other journalists intervened. The episode did Kieran's reputation no harm at all.

But I did not believe in stonewalling with the press. Nor did I believe that if a policy proved well-nigh impossible to explain, it should be defended to the bitter end. I was ill placed to argue with Christiane Amanpour about the need to act more decisively in Bosnia, because I agreed with her. My absolute rule was never to tell my friends in the press anything I wouldn't want to see published. But absent that, I told them as much as I could.

In Washington, the veteran columnist Joe Alsop was running out of steam, but had excellent stories of John Kennedy showing up at his house on the night of his inauguration to console the famous actress who was wailing that she might never see him again. Joe's rather nominal wife (they lived in separate houses and he was gay), Susan Mary, still could fit into the Dior dresses in which she had dazzled Duff Cooper and Paris in her youth.

The doyen of British correspondents in Washington was Henry Brandon, born in Czechoslovakia. Crossing the Atlantic on a merchant ship in the desperate summer of 1941, he was amazed on awaking one morning to find the convoy being escorted towards its US destination by American destroyers, giving him his first journalistic scoop. A supreme exponent of the access school of journalism, his most valuable source was Henry Kissinger, when Kissinger was Secretary of State. This did not prevent, and may have caused, Nixon arranging for his phone to be tapped. When Henry Brandon died, his last wish turned out to be a request to hold a commemorative party at the embassy for him, which we did.

This was followed by a party for grizzled veterans of the 82nd Airborne Division, who had parachuted back into Normandy to commemorate their landing there on D-Day. When I asked them about the experience, the response was, 'This time, we had to take our passports.'

For the *New York Times*, Johnny Apple, whether in London or Moscow, whenever he found the politics boring, would write inspiring articles about newly discovered restaurants in Manchester or Tbilisi. Other special friends included Tony Lewis for the *New York Times*; John Newhouse of the *New Yorker*, a formidable expert on arms control and one of the shrewdest observers of the Washington scene; Michael Beschloss; Jim Hoagland; and Martin Walker.

Many friends in the press helped me in the course of my career – Anthony Sampson with his friends in the ANC,

Simon Jenkins with his among the *verligte* academics in Stellenbosch, as well as Peter Jenkins and Hugo Young, writing for *The Guardian* in earlier days.

John Carlin was by far the shrewdest observer of Mandela. Other outstanding correspondents in South Africa were Patti Waldmeir, David Beresford and Joe Lelyveld. When I gave a party in Cape Town for the returning ANC exiles, they appeared impeccably dressed. Security, however, attempted to exclude three other invitees, alarmed at their dishevelled appearance. They turned out to be distinguished members of the British press.

In Washington, US Senators had the irritating habit of wanting to know who else was going to attend events at the embassy before deciding whether to do so themselves. This problem was solved by Barbara Walters, who turned up whenever appealed to. They would then show up too – seventeen of them on one occasion – in the vain hope that she would get around to interviewing them.

One of the pleasures of serving in Washington was a friendship with Christopher Hitchens, than whom no more entertaining company was to be found there. He asked me to help get Salman Rushdie an audience at the White House. I had known Christopher since his Trotskyite days. On moving to the US, due to his eloquence, humour and British accent, he became a prized exhibit on US television shows. He was impressed by their willingness to display iconoclastic views, showcased also in *Vanity Fair*.

When he wrote a benign article about me, because I had helped his idol Mandela, his friends were appalled. But he made up for it in the following week by launching an all-out attack on Mother Teresa.

Christopher both abhorred and admired Thatcher, regaling friends with his tale of the time when, following an argument in Parliament, she asked him to bend over – he claimed flirtatiously – and whacked him on the bottom with her order paper.

Christopher could recognise fascism when he saw it, specifically in the form of Islamo-fascism, which he believed needed to be confronted in both words and deeds. I miss to this day his clarity of mind, fierce independence and inexhaustible supply of accurate and hilarious aphorisms.

My most dependable and influential friend of all, helped by her addiction to playing tennis on the embassy court, was Katharine Graham. Invitations to innumerable events in her Georgetown mansion were an invaluable way of meeting half the political class. Talking to me one day about her friend Henry Kissinger, she observed, 'Some people say that Henry doesn't care about human rights. It isn't true. Henry *hates* human rights!'

Kissinger invited me to the main annual camp of the

Bohemian Grove amidst the magnificent redwood trees north of San Francisco. These log cabin gatherings were attended by half the captains of US industry and much of the Republican establishment. Summoned to perform at the David Rockefeller camp, we found ourselves required to do so in sombreros, with mariachis, accompanied by Herb Alpert and his Tijuana Brass. The San Francisco Symphony Orchestra performed a concert by the lake.

Kissinger was a great help to me in Washington. Seared by the experience of having to leave Germany in the 1930s, he believed and believes that the most important duty of a statesman is to manage relations with and between rival states, in his case with China and Russia, so as to avoid the inevitable rivalries leading into an extreme dangerous crisis. He stopped the 1973 war in the Middle East and extricated the US from Vietnam, for which he gets less credit than those who enmeshed the US there in the first place, and has maintained to this day access to the Chinese and Russian leaderships. His masterly study *Diplomacy* is unlikely to be bettered. The most intelligent of hawks, he was contemptuous of the neo-conservative advisers of George W. Bush who, he considered, combined dogmatism with a minimal understanding of realities in the Middle East.

When I wrote a study of Thatcher's foreign policy, he made a major contribution to it. Thatcher affected not to care what was written about her by most of the press and criticism bounced off her more readily than off others. John Major, being a decent and reasonable man, believed that if he spent hours talking to the press, they would support what he was trying to do. Christopher Meyer, as his press secretary, and I tried to disabuse him of this notion, both having been told by ungrateful hacks that he should have better things to do.

Long-serving foreign editors and correspondents of the kind I encountered have dwindled drastically in numbers today. I owe them a vote of thanks for the very real help they gave me at the time.

CHAPTER XXXI

A PARTING SHOT

Before leaving Washington, I had written a farewell despatch in the tradition publicised by Matthew Parris in his excellent collection of *Parting Shots*. This was deemed too sensitive to be published and when I asked to see it myself, most of it was redacted. In it, I argued for the kind of action that, a few weeks later, was taken against the Serbs.

I used it also to pursue another favourite cause. Visitors to Washington during my tenure had included Gordon Brown and Tony Blair. Jonathan Powell was put in charge of their programme. Gordon Brown, as shadow Chancellor, was clearly senior, but Blair made more of an impression both on us and on the Americans. We arranged for them to meet the Treasury Secretary, Lloyd Bentsen, and Alan Greenspan, head of the Federal Reserve. I asked both of them to impress on their visitors the advantages of central bank independence as a way of avoiding politically motivated interest rate decisions distorting management of the economy.

In my farewell despatch, I made the same argument, knowing that it was unlikely to appeal at the time to John Major, any more than it had to Margaret Thatcher, and certainly wouldn't to the Chancellor, Kenneth Clarke. But I was confident that this was an idea whose time would come and was pleased that this was one of the first decisions of the Blair government.

*   *   *

Before leaving Washington, I was invited to a farewell dinner by my friend and colleague the Saudi Ambassador, Prince Bandar. Bandar, who believed in doing things on a grand scale, told me there would be some entertainment. This turned out to be Roberta Flack and her band. The US foreign policy establishment then had to listen to Bandar declaring that he and I had always seen our duties in Washington in the same way. He proceeded to quote a better-left-forgotten Foreign Office memo from just after the war. Our task, it (and he) suggested, was 'to steer that great unwieldy barge, the United States, into a safe harbour. Otherwise it will continue to wallow in the ocean, an isolated hazard to navigation!'

There followed a farewell dinner at the embassy, attended by Margaret Thatcher, staying there at the time. Clinton's outstanding second Defense Secretary, Bill Perry, who had succeeded Les Aspin, read out what he knew to be one of my favourite Churchill quotes. 'The United States', he said, 'can be relied upon to do the right thing in the end, having first exhausted the available alternatives.'

In the case of Bosnia, this had been every bit as true of ourselves as of the Americans.

*   *   *

On my return to London, my closest friend in the Foreign Office hierarchy, the recently retired Permanent Under-Secretary, David Gillmore, told me that he had been asked by Blair to form a small group to advise him on the foreign policy issues he would face if he became Prime Minister. We met on Fridays at Blair's house in Islington. Other participants were Nico Henderson; David Simon, head of BP; David Hannay; and Rodric Braithwaite, formerly Ambassador in Moscow.

These were serious non-partisan sessions, with Blair keen to explore the issues. The one point of disagreement was about the euro, with most of the others keen on joining as soon as possible. In reality, Blair was too, but did not feel that he could say so going into an election. I could not see how this could work out any better for us than the ERM. Nor could I see how, within the eurozone, Italy and Greece could possibly hope to remain competitive with Germany.

At Blair's request, and with the agreement of the Conservative Defence Minister, Michael Portillo, I arranged a meeting for him with the head of the defence staff, Field Marshal Peter Inge, and his successor, General Charles Guthrie.

Immediately after Blair's victory in the election, David Hannay and I were summoned to a meeting with him and Gordon Brown before his first European summit. Our delegation in Brussels were suggesting that we might have to give up our border controls. If challenged by the Commission, they feared, we could suffer a defeat in the European Court of Justice. We said that as a newly elected Prime Minister with a large majority, he was well placed to declare that we regarded these as vital for us.

Following the election, I was asked via Jonathan Powell if I would support the government on foreign policy in the House of Lords. I agreed to do so, though not to vote on most domestic issues. I did so because I supported the attempt by Blair to turn the Labour Party into a British version of the US Democratic Party, as a viable centrist alternative government.

I continue to believe that this country would have been better off if he had succeeded. Blair did not seem to me to have a socialist bone in his body. This proved to be a deficiency for which his party never forgave him. Though he won three elections, it was a short-lived project. When Gordon Brown succeeded him, I moved to the crossbenches.

CHAPTER XXXII

WHEN ATLAS SHRUGS

The turning inward of the United States was a natural reaction to the botched invasion of Iraq and long drawn-out conflict in Afghanistan. It was not Donald Trump but Barack Obama who first challenged head-on the notion of the United States as the 'indispensable nation' in dealing with international crises. Obama was explicit that he did not want to see the United States continuing to take on this role. He and his deputy national security adviser, Ben Rhodes, spent time at war with the US national security community, Democratic as well as Republican, which they referred to as 'The Blob'.

Obama regarded the war in Syria as a matter for the Europeans, though he did declare a 'red line' against the use of chemical weapons. When several hundred people were killed in the chemical weapons attack in Damascus in August 2013, abetted by a negative vote in the House of Commons, Obama decided to ignore his own red line – to the dismay of his Secretary of State, Defense Secretary and 'The Blob'. This proved to be a very expensive mistake, emboldening Putin, first in Syria, then in Ukraine.

Obama initially dismissed the Islamic State as just a 'junior varsity team', and the US campaign against the Islamic State was pursued only very cautiously, until taken over under Trump by General Mattis. Through the use of special forces and air strikes guided by forward air controllers, Mattis helped the Iraqi and free Syrian forces to recover huge swathes of territory from IS, ousting them from their strongholds in Mosul and Raqqa and rendering the 'caliphate' a dramatically shrunken version of itself. Regarded as the main stabilising factor in the Trump administration, Mattis resigned in December 2018 in protest at Trump's decision to end US military involvement in Syria.

*   *   *

So what is the significance of Donald Trump and how much damage is he likely to cause? His decision about Syria, announced in a tweet with no consultation with America's allies, has shown how temperamentally unfitted he is to be commander in chief. The world has been shocked by the re-emergence of an erratic and often incoherent throwback to the doctrines of America First, tempered by Congressional hostility to Russia under Putin and attachment to NATO. The effect has been to weaken relationships with the allies and America's standing in the world.

But Congress is just as critical as Trump of the failure of the European allies to do more to help defend themselves.

It is a really serious aberration, three quarters of a century after the Second World War, that Germany should still be spending so little on its own defence and that its forces should be in so poor a state of readiness. US Defense Secretaries regard NATO as a two-tier alliance, in which only Britain and France can offer effective military support.

President Macron chose the centenary of the Armistice ending the First World War to talk of the need for Europe to create its own army 'to protect us vis à-vis China, Russia *and even the United States*'. Among the many justifiably derided statements of Donald Trump, it is hard to think of one much sillier than this. Angela Merkel joined in advocating the creation of a 'real' European army, despite the current extraordinary state of unpreparedness of the German armed forces, which has become a political scandal in Germany, and the constitutional constraints on their engaging in any meaningful military action.

The EU at present has neither the unity, the military or logistic capacity nor the political will to create a worthwhile system of European defence, and European governments are extremely unlikely to make the financial and other sacrifices that would be necessary to establish one. It is their membership of NATO and the collective defence provisions of the NATO treaty that have curbed Putin's ambitions vis-à-vis the Baltic states, and little else – an opinion strongly held by their citizens and those of the rest of eastern Europe. What may end up being created is liable to be the appearance but not the substance of a European 'army'.

Many in Congress would be delighted if the Europeans chose to defend themselves. They should be careful not to create the dangerous illusion that they actually intend to do so.

In North Korea, Trump has got nowhere near persuading Kim Jong-un to denuclearise, but a combination of US military preparedness and serious pressure from China has interrupted the nuclear and long-range missile testing programmes which posed the threat of provoking a major crisis.

* * *

The one certainty about Trump's trade wars is that they are bound to be damaging to the world economy. But the $350 billion surplus in Chinese trade with the US is unprecedented in world history. Despite admission to the

World Trade Organization, China has done little to open up its own economy to foreign investors, while continuing to insist on forced technology transfer and engage in technological espionage. At an investor conference in Shanghai pre-Trump, I and others argued that unless China opened up its own market, which clearly was the better course, it would risk facing retaliation. Most of the Chinese speakers agreed and President Xi made some initial promises to this effect in his first meeting with Trump in Florida.

Trump's policy towards China, alone among his policies, has bipartisan support. The highly intelligent Chinese leadership know that they can ill afford an all-out economic conflict with the United States. In a subsequent meeting with Trump, President Xi promised major additional imports from the US, plus action on forced technology transfer and theft and cyber-attacks. It remains to be seen how meaningful these measures will turn out to be, but Trump is likely to be able to claim a measure of success in this conflict at some point.

The US will not revert to acting as the 'indispensable nation' if it can get no allied support. Trump did secure British and French support for the action in Syria. Nor is it sensible to seek to avoid acknowledging that on NATO burden-sharing, on Iran's continuing efforts to destabilise the Middle East and on the effects of globalisation on blue-collar workers in the US (and elsewhere), he has a point.

Trump's apparent obsession with illegal immigration has been denounced by all right-thinking commentators, the only problem being that most Americans appear to agree with him, though not with his government shutdown. Immigration is an issue most western governing elites have found it hard to grapple with for fear of being branded uncaring and racist. But net migration of 600,000 into the United Kingdom in the year before the referendum on the EU will have affected the outcome of the vote, and the presence of over half a million migrants in Italy is weighing very heavily on politics there. Economic migrants, with the increasing involvement of people traffickers, have become habituated to claiming to be refugees or asylum seekers. An unacknowledged problem in the United Kingdom is that a key reason why migrants try so hard to cross the whole of Europe to arrive on our shores is that the benefits system is non-contributory, whereas in many of our neighbours, benefits cannot be claimed without a prior contribution. As the population of sub-Saharan Africa is forecast to increase by a further billion people by the 2050s, the ability or failure to control mass migration across its borders will be crucial for the future of the European Union.

Trump has had his wings seriously clipped by the loss to the Democrats of control over the House of

Representatives. Nor, despite nominating a new head of the Federal Reserve Board, has he had, and nor will he have, much success in persuading them not to raise interest rates. Americans have a liking for divided government, are undismayed by gridlock and frequently vote for it. They are less inclined than Europeans to see government as a solution to their problems (*l'état providence*) and would prefer it to take the Hippocratic oath: 'First do no harm.' Trump will continue to find his more extreme measures contested by the judiciary and will meanwhile be enmeshed in serious judicial problems of his own. The danger of an unfettered Trump presidency has always been remote.

While the departure of General Mattis has demonstrated that neither Britain nor any other ally can rely on the erratic President, the institutional links that underpin the relationship remain in place. The economic links are as close and the cross-investments as large as they have ever been. When Trump flirted with Putin, the Republican leader in the Senate, Mitch McConnell, declared, 'NATO *is* important; and the Russians [under Putin] are *not* our friends.' The Senate led the way in imposing punitive sanctions on Russia following the poisoning in Britain of the former Russian military intelligence agent Sergei Skripal. The Pentagon at all levels will oppose any weakening of the ties with America's principal allies, as will the US intelligence community and those engaged in cooperation with the UK on nuclear weapons.

Dealing with this erratic presidency is going to require the exercise of strategic patience. In his resignation letter, General Mattis defended the role of the US as the 'indispensable nation', with both sides in the Senate supporting him, which is just as well, as the US remains as vital as ever to the defence of Europe and the defeat of the Islamic State and Al Qaeda.

Trump was lucky to win the last election, despite polling fewer votes than Hillary Clinton. His apparently improbable victory was the result of a white revolt. According to her pollster, the only category of white Americans in which Hillary was ahead was among those with PhDs. He may need to be even luckier to win the next one, provided the Democrats choose a candidate who can appeal to centrist voters (though that is by no means a given). Given the checks and balances in the US constitution, the Trump presidency is very unlikely to mark 'the end of NATO' or of a generally positive relationship with Britain.

Despite goodwill towards us on both sides of Congress, including on the part of the new Speaker, Nancy Pelosi, our standing in Washington at present is not high, because of the perceived weakness of the government, uncertainty over what future capacity we will have to negotiate a trade agreement with the US and the continued shrinkage and underfunding of our armed forces. Many of the massive US investments in Britain have been made to help gain duty-free access to the rest of the European market. Whatever Trump's personal views, successive US administrations have attached importance to the influence we could exert within the European Union to help counter transatlantic drift and the development of serious divergences over security and trade. Our influence in Washington has depended to a significant degree on our influence in Europe. The US will reach its own judgement on the relative success or failure of Britain and its economy post-Brexit.

CHAPTER XXXIII

WARS OF CHOICE

While the United States wrestles with the extent to which it should continue to play the role of 'indispensable nation' in helping to deal with international crises, Britain faces some similar choices itself.

My friend and colleague Richard Haass held senior positions in the State Department and on the National Security Council staff in the Reagan, Bush Sr and Bush Jr administrations. Under George W. Bush, he opposed the rush to war in Iraq. He is today president of the Council of Foreign Relations in New York.

Following the extremely costly US and allied interventions in Afghanistan and Iraq, he published a book, *War of Necessity, War of Choice*, in which he argued that the intervention in Afghanistan was a war of necessity. The Taliban, having hosted Osama bin Laden and his Al Qaeda colleagues throughout the planning for the 9/11 attacks, could not be allowed to remain in control of

Afghanistan. For the security of the west, it was vital to remove them.

There ensued an interminable conflict, which continues today. Those who believe, however, that we have become expert at *Losing Small Wars* need to explain how it is that eighteen years after the initial intervention, a pro-western government remains in control in Kabul and the other major centres. An extremely threatening Taliban insurgency continues, with Islamic State also trying hard to establish footholds there, but no further terrorist operations in the west have been conducted from Afghanistan. Trump would like to draw down the US forces there, but will need to be careful. There will be no prizes in the US for the President who, after all these efforts, 'loses' Afghanistan.

As for the war in Iraq, Haass argued then, and today, there can be no real dispute that it was a war of choice. It did not look that way to Tony Blair, who was persuaded that Saddam Hussein really did have active chemical and biological weapons programmes and who believed anyway that the world would be a better place without Saddam Hussein. Having also been assured at the time by a senior figure in MI6 that the regime had eighteen mobile biological weapons laboratories and chemical weapons ready for battlefield use, I asked how much of this intelligence came from the Iraqi exiles. The response was that there was plenty of collateral from other sources, which turned out to be a straightforward untruth.

For the US neo-conservatives who were ardent advocates of the invasion, the war was fought on the equally false premise that Iraq thereafter could be turned into some sort of western-style democracy. As Kissinger observed to me at the time, 'The trouble with the neo-conservatives is that they are not conservatives at all.'

Wars of necessity are fought because national security interests are clearly seen or believed to be at stake.

The crisis in Bosnia posed a different kind of dilemma. The horrors of the war were displayed nightly on western news programmes, leading to demands, in Douglas Hurd's words, that 'something must be done'. For a long time, military action was eschewed by the US and others because no national security threat appeared to exist. Those advocating more forceful action were doing so on humanitarian grounds. In the event, it proved possible to stop the war in Bosnia without the loss of a single allied soldier.

A similar success in Kosovo led Blair, in his speech in Chicago in 1999, to articulate a new doctrine of humanitarian intervention, justifying military action when no national interests appeared to be involved.

Kissinger was horrified, seeing this as liable to lead over time to multiple interventions with uncertain outcomes, not justified by the need to protect national interests.

The intervention in Libya, which also entailed no allied casualties, succeeded in saving the rebels in Benghazi threatened with extermination by Gaddafi, but morphed into regime change, with no thought or planning for the aftermath. The Americans, who took a lot of persuading to intervene, made clear that subsequent nation-building was going to be left to the Europeans, who made wholly inadequate efforts to address it.

While it was justifiable to intervene in Bosnia and Kosovo, where the risks were calculated and successful exits could be managed, the Libyan experience should have a salutary effect in causing those who feel strongly that something must be done to think through more carefully the consequences of actually doing it. Meeting the relatives of young soldiers killed in action, it is harder to justify their sacrifice unless it was in response to a direct threat to this country.

But the price of doing nothing also can be extremely serious. When the Syrian regime launched the chemical weapons attack killing thousands of people in Damascus, David Cameron's decision to seek prior parliamentary approval for British participation in a Cruise missile strike on the Republican Guard base from which the attack had been launched contributed to a fiasco and was self-defeating, as, in cases of this kind, delay enables the target to avoid the retaliation. When, years later, Trump did authorise air strikes, with UK and French support, to deter the Syrian regime from continuing to use poison gas, Theresa May reverted to the practice of accounting to Parliament, but after the event.

While some experts queried what difference our very modest military contribution could make to what has turned out to be a pretty successful campaign against the Islamic State in Syria, this is to misunderstand the dynamics in Washington. The willingness of a key ally to act with the US will always be important to the administration and to Congress. From this perspective, by committing so early to take action come what might, Blair was felt by some major figures in Washington to have underestimated his leverage there in the run-up to the Iraq War.

We are very unlikely in future to have to engage in a serious conflict on our own, as we did in the Falklands War. But even with Donald Trump, the willingness of Britain and France to participate was a contributing factor to the action the US at last took to deter the use of chemical weapons by the regime in Syria. A willingness to act in such cases, when justified, with our key allies will remain crucial to our standing and influence in the world. Acceptance of the view of those in Parliament who contend that Britain should never take military action without the prior approval of the United Nations would mean that we would never again be able to do so without the permission of Russia and China. If that were to be the doctrine adopted by us, the world would be the poorer for it.

CHAPTER XXXIV

HOTEL CALIFORNIA

Clement Attlee regarded referendums as a 'device of dictators and demagogues'. Thatcher was equally scathing about them, until her declining years. In their view, on complex and difficult issues, it was for government to set out its policy and for Parliament and the electorate to approve it or not.

David Cameron, a tactician rather than a strategist, proposed this blunt instrument as a way of countering the UK Independence Party and of managing, at any rate temporarily, the divisions within his party, notwithstanding the fact that, in the event, the effect has been to envenom them. He did so in the over-confident expectation that his persuasive powers would convince the British people to vote to remain.

A rational argument for leaving the EU can be made by those who want to see the United Kingdom governed from Westminster, rather than ever increasingly from

Brussels. The hyper-bureaucratic nature of the EU and the attempt to link Germany and much weaker member states in a single-currency zone has rendered it dysfunctional in many respects, resulting in sky-high youth unemployment in the southern member states.

The word 'deregulation' is not supposed to be used in Brussels; it is permissible only to talk in terms of 'better regulation.' The Commission is a regulatory machine and Europe has become the most heavily regulated corner of the planet. At the same time, and not coincidentally, Europe's output has declined from 30 per cent to around 15 per cent of world GDP. The effect of this increasing mass of regulation is to favour large companies, which can better afford the legal, compliance and technological costs, at the expense of small companies, which are the main employment creators.

But Brexiteers have fatally underestimated the difficulty of getting from where we are now to where they want to be. For the course of the Brexit negotiations has given definitively the lie to those in the referendum campaign who contended that leaving would be easy and scot-free. Boris Johnson and other Brexiteers would have done their reputations a great deal more good if they had had the honesty and political courage to acknowledge that leaving would be difficult and costly, whatever the real or supposed benefits thereafter. When British negotiators suggested that the objective should be a 'win–win', the Commission poured scorn on the idea. The EU had to be seen to have won *pour décourager les autres*.

And so it turned out. The government committed the folly of triggering Article 50, setting the clock ticking for our departure, with no effective preliminary soundings in Brussels and no idea as to how the negotiation might turn out. A full Brexit, taking us out of the jurisdiction of the EU, entailed the negotiation of a free trade agreement, which was scarcely entered into, so preoccupied were the UK negotiators with avoiding a cliff-edge exit by the deadline they had imposed on themselves. They were bound also to find that, in a free trade agreement, the Commission still would be trying to insist on regulatory alignment and a separate regime for Northern Ireland. While the government did secure an end to the free movement of people to and from the EU (though this in general has been beneficial for the British economy), the withdrawal agreement left the UK subject to all EU laws and regulations, a 'backstop' to ensure no hard border in Ireland, and a 'divorce' payment of €39 billion.

The Prime Minister's principal negotiator warned that the so-called Irish backstop was 'bad for Britain' and that the effect could be an inability ever to exit the customs union. In the real world, the backstop is a partly theoretical problem, as, whatever form Brexit takes, it is hard to imagine either the British or the Irish government seeking to re-establish physical controls on the Northern Ireland border and the resultant degree of economic leakage could be limited by actions away from the border. The Commission has used it to argue that either the whole of the UK must remain in the customs union or, at least, Northern Ireland must do so. Forced by Parliament to publish his advice, the Attorney General confirmed the 'absence of a right of termination' without the agreement of the EU. If the purpose of the negotiating team had been to demonstrate the advantages of remaining, they could not have done a better job.

The concern of the Commission has been that if no longer required to accept all EU regulations, the UK could end up with a more competitive economy. As they made clear in briefing the other member states, their objective is to oblige the UK to accept a long-term alignment with EU rules. 'This requires the customs union as the basis of the future relationship. They must align their rules, but the EU will retain all the controls.' (*The Times*, 14 November 2018.)

In their version of Hotel California, 'you can check out, but you can never leave'. The Commission will continue to insist on a 'dynamic' future alignment with EU regulation as the price of unfettered access to the single market. On the Attorney General's assessment that the United Kingdom in the future could not leave the customs union without the permission of the EU, the *Financial Times* observed in November 2018 that 'such a veto is intolerable for the world's fifth largest economy'.

In June 2016, just over half of those who cast their ballot voted to leave the European Union, just under half voted to stay, but no one voted to leave while remaining indefinitely subject to EU laws and regulations over which we will no longer have any say, with no exit possible without the permission of the EU. Yet the no exit feature without EU permission was approved by the Prime Minister, while rejecting demands for a second vote on the Orwellian grounds that this would be 'undemocratic'.

As a former negotiator with the EU, albeit for a very different Prime Minister, there is no way I would ever have signed such a document without a guaranteed exit clause. The worst mistake any negotiator can make is to conclude an agreement formally approved at the highest level, then try to change it. As the EU would not do so, it duly was defeated in the House of Commons by over 200 votes, but with the Prime Minister still sticking to it or something very like it.

The hardline Brexiteers, prepared to see Britain exit with no agreement, number only around eighty in the House of Commons. So this could only happen by default, leading to moves by others in Parliament to seek an extension to the Article 50 deadline. The leader of the opposition, a committed Brexiteer, determined to thwart demands in his party for a new referendum, refused to discuss with the government any way out of this impasse. But the Prime Minister is just as responsible for the failure to seek any cross-party support. Her agreement would be viable, though only in the near term, if she could get the no guaranteed exit clause effectively withdrawn. As she tries to make the 'backstop' disappear, her strategy remains to wind down the clock until, she hopes, a chastened Parliament votes for some version of her agreement.

The opposition parties would prefer longer-term membership of the customs union, which would overcome the Northern Ireland problem, but would put paid to any notion of an independent trade policy and produce an explosion in the Conservative Party. The so-called Norway option would entail continued free movement, plus contributions to the EU budget, though it does allow an exit. Given that the outcome will affect this country's future for decades, a sane alternative would be to hold another, better-informed referendum, opposed by both Corbyn and May. None of these courses of action as yet commands a clear majority in Parliament. The risk is obvious of a muddled outcome, a 'Brexit in name only', that may end up satisfying neither Remainers nor Brexiteers.

Future historians are unlikely to be kind about the quality of leadership displayed by any of the principal actors in this saga. As the United Kingdom ties itself in knots over Brexit, the world outside our borders has been looking on with amazement at this self-defeating performance by the supposedly sensible and pragmatic British.

For the long-suffering citizens of these islands, the desire increasingly will be to get it over with, whereupon they will find that the sky has not fallen in and that the situation post-Brexit may bear a strange resemblance to what it was before.

CHAPTER XXXV

'IS HE LUCKY?'

*Question supposed to be asked by Napoleon before appointing
one of his generals. The question also was asked by Cardinal
Mazarin, Chief Minister of France 1642–61.*

I enjoyed a lot of sheer good luck in my diplomatic
career. Our intervention in the Rhodesia crisis could
have ended a lot less well for us than it did. A less resolute
Prime Minister would have gone along with Haig's efforts
to engineer a barely disguised transfer of the Falklands
to Argentina. Correcting the British contribution to the
budget resolved what was at the time the main grievance
in our relationship with the European Community. The
subsequent negotiation opened up the European market
to us in services, which will be affected by Brexit.

It was extremely good fortune to serve in South Africa
when F. W. de Klerk, a friend to this day, took the courageous decisions he did and Nelson Mandela, on his release

from prison, decided that he needed our help. Frustrated at our failure to do so earlier, I was relieved that my last weeks in Washington coincided with the US-led decision at last to take conclusive action to end the Bosnian War.

This was a period in which, in my opinion, Britain made a positive difference in world affairs. Certainly we did so in southern Africa, in helping to end the Rhodesian and Namibian wars and to encourage a dramatic turnaround in South Africa.

* * *

I was fortunate to serve in Washington at a time when, under both a Republican and a Democratic President, our influence and access there, including to the President, was greater than that of other countries. This did not mean, and never could, that they would necessarily agree with us.

Our exit from the European Union will constrain in important ways our position in the world. The Americans and others placed a lot of value on our influence within it. But it will not nullify the role we can play in trying to help make the world a safer place than it would be if free rein were given to Putin and his allies or if we failed to help deal with the threat posed by the so-called Islamic State and Al Qaeda. That in turn will depend on governments devoting more resources to our reduced but still greatly admired armed forces. Failing that, we really must expect in future to find our influence shrinking too and debates in Parliament about world affairs will risk becoming increasingly irrelevant.

That is a denouement that can be avoided, but it will require skill and determination to do so, not just windy rhetoric about the opportunities in the wider world, which existed anyway.

Post-Brexit, we will be engaged in a permanent negotiation with the European Union, though henceforth from outside it. It will require skill to defend our interests in that dialogue too and to continue to act as one of the ties that bind Europe and the United States together.

Our exit is not the end of the world, still less the end of foreign policy. Our success or relative decline after leaving will depend on whether we succeed in making this country more enterprise-friendly than most of our European counterparts, as we still are today. That is an achievable goal, if we have governments committed to achieving it. For the British economy to date has proved remarkably resilient. Unemployment is at half the level in France, where taxation now amounts to 49 per cent of GDP and President Macron's reforms appear seriously compromised in the face of the resistance of the *gilets jaunes*.

At which point, let me cease to be diplomatic. Having watched with disbelief the self-defeating contortions of the Conservative Party, it nevertheless is the case that if we wish to deepen dramatically further the perceptible loss in our influence and standing in the world, the solution will be to elect Jeremy Corbyn. He has always been a Brexiteer, because he wants to return to the state aid policies that proved so futile in the 1970s, which the European Commission would no longer allow. The Labour Party position that, on leaving, we must enjoy the 'exact same benefits' as we have as members of the EU is self-evidently absurd.

Anti-Americanism has long been a feature of the left (and some on the right) in Britain, but not hitherto of its leadership. Having burned a lot of bridges in Europe, we will then have succeeded in burning them with America too. We will have as much say in world affairs as, say, Italy. MPs would then be better able to concentrate on their constituencies, as, on any international issue, no one outside these shores would be listening to a word they said. If such a government does come to power, I doubt if it will endure.

So I hope that this account of my adventures in the foreign service will encourage others to consider joining it. They should only do so if their families are prepared to accept the stresses and disruption of this itinerant lifestyle and to make as important a contribution to their success as mine did for me.

If they do, I would urge them to bear in mind my

conviction that nearly every crisis creates an opportunity, discrediting conventional wisdom and demanding fresh thinking. Also that there is particular satisfaction in working for one's country and those who do may find themselves working with as remarkable an array of colleagues as it was my good fortune to do.

ACKNOWLEDGEMENTS

I am extremely grateful to Olivia Beattie, James Stephens and the team at Biteback for all their help with and support for this memoir, and to Professor Patrick Salmon, chief historian in the Foreign and Commonwealth Office, for his comments and for kindly arranging for me to be able to consult some of my reports.

I am grateful to Sue Charlton for kindly retrieving some photographs from my time in South Africa; and to Douglas Cooper and Marie-France Renwick for their help with the manuscript.

I owed a particular debt in Washington to my remarkable private secretary, Karen Pierce, who is today our Permanent Representative to the United Nations; and to the social secretary, Amanda Downes, who has done much to enhance the reputation of the embassy, including acting as a part-time adviser to the White House!

My thanks above all are due to the colleagues who served

with me in the Foreign and Commonwealth Office, in the United States and in South Africa, without whose efforts this would not have been a story worth telling.

INDEX